Barcode in Back

Google AdWords

D1710134

Anastasia Holdren

HUMBER LIBRARIES LAKESHORE CAMPUS
3199 Lakeshore Blvd West
TORONTO, ON.   M8V 1K8

O'REILLY®

Beijing · Cambridge · Farnham · Köln · Sebastopol · Tokyo

X

Google AdWords

by Anastasia Holdren

Copyright © 2012 SEM Training LLC. All rights reserved.
Printed in the United States of America.

Published by O'Reilly Media, Inc., 1005 Gravenstein Highway North, Sebastopol, CA 95472.

O'Reilly books may be purchased for educational, business, or sales promotional use. Online editions are also available for most titles (*http://my.safaribooksonline.com*). For more information, contact our corporate/institutional sales department: (800) 998-9938 or *corporate@oreilly.com*.

Editors: Simon St. Laurent and Courtney Nash
Production Editor: Teresa Elsey

Cover Designer: Karen Montgomery
Interior Designer: David Futato
Illustrator: Robert Romano

Revision History for the First Edition:
2011-11-01   First release
2012-06-28   Second release
See *http://oreilly.com/catalog/errata.csp?isbn=9781449308384* for release details.

Nutshell Handbook, the Nutshell Handbook logo, and the O'Reilly logo are registered trademarks of O'Reilly Media, Inc. *Google AdWords*, the image of a spotted goby, and related trade dress are trademarks of O'Reilly Media, Inc.

Many of the designations used by manufacturers and sellers to distinguish their products are claimed as trademarks. Where those designations appear in this book, and O'Reilly Media, Inc., was aware of a trademark claim, the designations have been printed in caps or initial caps.

While every precaution has been taken in the preparation of this book, the publisher and author assume no responsibility for errors or omissions, or for damages resulting from the use of the information contained herein.

ISBN: 978-1-449-30838-4

[LSI]

1340972304

For Cameron and Scott—thanks, guys.

Table of Contents

Foreword

Have you been online today?

Unless you live in the confines of a cave still not serviced by cellular or satellite, and regardless what day of the week or how early in the morning you might be reading this, the answer is very likely a resounding "Yes, I have." But it wasn't that long ago that car phones resembled NASA equipment fit for a mission to Mars and the Internet was something experienced on the family desktop computer, once everyone was done using the telephone for anything else.

Well, the world has changed, and with that change has come a veritable new frontier for the field of marketing. At the turn of the 20th century, John Wanamaker famously said, "I fully believe that half the money I spend on marketing is wasted. The trouble is, I don't know which half." And therein lies the fundamental problem of traditional marketing, which we've struggled to overcome since before Mr. Wanamaker uttered his famous words.

We've put our messages on the pages of newspapers and magazines, sent them out over the airwaves of radio, and made them dance in front of the eyeballs glued to the living room television. We've paid the postage for our mail drops, we've listed ourselves in all the colors of directory pages, and we've purchased lists of potential consumers of our products and services. And in the end, we've put forth our best, most educated guesses, and we've been left hoping that our target market just happens to be on the receiving end of our messages, just when they need us most.

But back to our question: *Why* were you online today? If you weren't checking your email, then, most likely, you were searching for something. And to an advertiser, that means you were exposing your *intent*; you were telling the marketers, in your own words, *exactly* what you wanted *at that very moment*. If only we as advertisers could get our hands on you right when you did that search...

... and that is exactly what Google AdWords has enabled us to do. As you read through this book, you'll see that we no longer need to guess, and we no longer need to waste our advertising dollars on prospects that have no interest in our products and services. If you're selling, say, sandwiches, then you're trying your hardest to seek out all those people who are hungry right now, actively on the prowl to solve that problem of theirs with a sandwich. Wouldn't you love to be there just when someone nearby types "sandwich shop" into their phone so you could jump out with a big sign promoting your sandwiches? Well, that's exactly what we're doing here.

And it gets better than that. Not only can we go after our potential customers by the words they type, but also AdWords allows us to further refine our targeting by things like geography, device, day of week, time of day, networks, websites, demographics, and even interests that users have displayed as they traverse the Web. Wanna offer up a coupon to hungry people interested in food who are searching from a smartphone or a tablet using a signal from a wireless carrier somewhere within 5 miles of your location, only during your hours of operation? This book will show you how.

And how about scale? Through this platform, you can reach more than 80 percent of the entire Internet-using world, showing your ads across the Google properties that have become a staple of our everyday lives, as well as more than *a million other websites*. And all of this is available in an advertising medium that is remarkably accountable. Through flexible bidding options and the tracking mechanisms you'll learn about, through AdWords and tools like Google Analytics, you'll finally be able to control your costs, measure impact, and calculate the return on your advertising investment within a matter of hours of launching your campaigns.

Excited yet? You should be. The bottom line is that Google AdWords has seen such enormous success for one simple reason: for most advertisers, and in most situations, with an understanding of the tool and the right management, *it just plain works*. And this book is a foundational step towards refining or developing an AdWords strategy that works for you as well.

I met Stasia for the first time while on the road as a fellow Google Seminars for Success Leader, and it was immediately apparent that she was truly passionate about showing people how to take full advantage of this opportunity. It goes without saying that she maintains a vast array of knowledge and experience on the topic, but much more importantly, Stasia possesses that rare gift for being able to gracefully and effectively impart a practical—and usable—understanding of it to others.

In the years that have followed, I've had the pleasure of working with Stasia all around the world and seeing this firsthand. In every seminar, at every event, during every training, and inside every consultation, I have watched as she has proven this ability without fail, leaving behind a fresh wave of newly empowered marketers. As you'll see in the pages of this book, Stasia's ability to teach in person translates impeccably well to print, and you couldn't be in better hands when learning how to make Google AdWords work for you.

So whether you're a seasoned veteran looking to brush up your skills or if this is a new journey you're about to begin, get ready—you're about to find the other half of that marketing budget!

—David Booth
Senior Partner, Cardinal Path, and Google Seminars for Success Leader, AdWords, Analytics, Urchin, and Website Optimizer Certified Partner

Preface

Since being selected as an AdWords Seminar Leader by Google in 2006, I've had the opportunity to teach thousands of businesses and organizations how to use AdWords, Google's advertising platform. I believe in the product; if used appropriately, it offers vast online exposure for advertisers. Unfortunately, most advertisers do not understand how AdWords works or hold it accountable to deliver value to their businesses. Some advertisers make money by dumb luck; others waste hundreds or thousands of dollars each month. I've met countless advertisers who gauge the effectiveness of their online campaigns based on gut feelings. I'm generally a proponent of trusting one's gut, but not in the case of online advertising. In this world, it's all about the data.

It's in Google's best interests for advertisers to use data to make decisions about their campaigns. If AdWords is working for a business, and the numbers prove it, that business is likely to continue advertising and potentially allocate more of its budget to AdWords. Conversely, advertisers can use this data to identify what's not working, so they can try something else or stop wasting money.

The AdWords platform includes free, simple tools to track and measure performance, down to the individual keyword level. This book is intended to help new and existing advertisers improve the quality of their advertising campaigns and quantify the value AdWords brings to their businesses.

So why Google AdWords? Why not other viable online advertising options like Bing or Facebook? No reason; you should try them all. Everyone has to start somewhere, and AdWords is the logical choice considering the popularity of search and Google's impressive market share of search volume, as seen in Figure P-1.

With AdWords you'll get a lot of bang for your buck ("bang" measured by potential ad exposure, "buck" by the effort and expenditure of setting up and managing campaigns).

In my classes I encourage businesses to promote themselves wherever target customers spend their time online. You may be able to get cheaper clicks or better conversion rates for some keywords on different advertising platforms, but Google AdWords provides the volume necessary to grow your business.

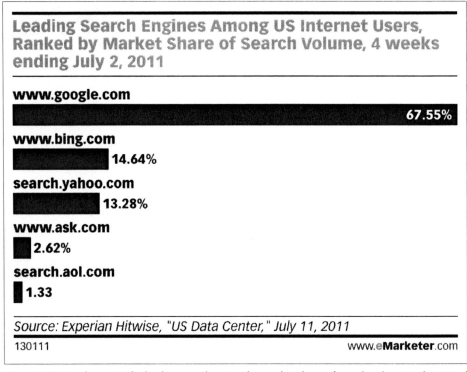

Figure P-1. Google.com is the leading search engine by market share of search volume in the United States, according to Experian Hitwise "US Data Center" from July 11, 2011, provided by eMarketer.

I've heard this question at every class I've taught for the past five years: do searchers *really* click on ads? It's an understandable question, because it's difficult to imagine search behavior differing from your own. If you always gravitate to Google's organic results, you might assume ads are irrelevant.

Google's 2011 annual report disproves this assumption. Gross revenue was $37,905,000,000, and 96 percent of this was advertising revenue derived from Ad-Words and display advertising. In the first quarter of 2012, Google reported revenues of $10.65 billion, a 24 percent increase compared to the first quarter of 2011. The numbers prove that people do indeed notice and click on ads to find products, services, or information they are looking for.

According to the digital research company eMarketer, growth for U.S. online ad spending continues to rise. As you can see in Figure P-2, search is the leading category, claiming close to half of online ad spending. Total online ad spending will approach $49.5 billion by 2015.

This is not to say that paid advertising is the best option for promoting a business online. After all, who doesn't want free exposure from the organic results? The process of optimizing for organic results is called search engine optimization (SEO), and this book

US Online Ad Spending, by Format, 2010-2015

billions

	2010	2011	2012	2013	2014	2015
Search	$12.00	$14.38	$17.03	$18.85	$20.19	$21.53
Banner ads	$6.23	$7.61	$8.94	$9.93	$10.97	$11.73
Classifieds and directories	$2.60	$3.00	$3.35	$3.65	$3.98	$4.29
Video	$1.42	$2.16	$3.09	$4.20	$5.64	$7.11
Rich media	$1.54	$1.66	$1.73	$1.74	$1.73	$1.68
Lead generation	$1.34	$1.42	$1.45	$1.47	$1.50	$1.52
Sponsorships	$0.72	$0.91	$1.05	$1.18	$1.32	$1.47
Email	$0.20	$0.16	$0.16	$0.17	$0.17	$0.18
Total	**$26.04**	**$31.30**	**$36.80**	**$41.20**	**$45.50**	**$49.50**

Source: eMarketer, June 2011

128163   www.**eMarketer**.com

Figure P-2. U.S. online ad spending 2010-2015

doesn't cover it. Google's organic algorithm is completely separate from AdWords, and ad spending does not influence organic position in any way.

If high placement in the organic results is your primary objective, AdWords may still prove useful. If you are not sure which keywords to focus on for SEO, you can use AdWords to test and identify profitable keywords. It may take months of work before your website ranks well organically on the selected keywords; in the meantime, AdWords can provide interim exposure. Many businesses do both, because a bigger presence on the search results page improves the chance of connecting with a searcher.

No matter which advertising route you choose, the objective remains the same: help potential customers find your website. In this book, I show you how to connect with potential customers and spend your advertising budget wisely. My teaching philosophy is to keep it short and sweet; this book packs a great deal of AdWords information as succinctly as possible. I hope it helps existing advertisers fine-tune their accounts and new advertisers get off to the right start.

Terminology Used in This Book

If you are new to AdWords and online advertising, there are many terms to familiarize yourself with. The following list covers the most common terms used in online advertising, which are used throughout the book. Refer to the Glossary at the end of this book for a comprehensive list of terms and definitions.

AdWords
  The brand name for Google's advertising platform. There is no such thing as an "AdWord."

Clickthrough rate (CTR)
  The number of clicks on an ad divided by the number of times the ad is displayed (impressions), expressed as a percentage.

Conversion
  When a click on an ad results in a desirable behavior, like an online purchase.

Impression
  The appearance of an ad on a search results page, whether someone clicks on it or not.

Keyword
  A word or phrase that can trigger an ad on a search engine results page. A keyword is not an AdWord.

Search engine results page (SERP)
  The page presented to a searcher after typing a search query into a search engine.

Search query
  The word or phrase a searcher types into a search engine.

Conventions Used in This Book

The following typographical conventions are used in this book:

Italic
  Indicates new terms, URLs, email addresses, filenames, and file extensions.

`Constant width`
  Used for program listings, as well as within paragraphs to refer to program elements such as variable or function names, databases, data types, environment variables, statements, and keywords.

`Constant width bold`
  Shows commands or other text that should be typed literally by the user.

`Constant width italic`
  Shows text that should be replaced with user-supplied values or by values determined by context.

This icon signifies a tip, suggestion, or general note.

 This icon indicates a warning or caution.

Attribution and Permissions

This book is here to help you get your job done. If you reference limited parts of it in your work or writings, we appreciate, but do not require, attribution. An attribution usually includes the title, author, publisher, and ISBN. For example: "*Google AdWords* by Anastasia Holdren (O'Reilly). Copyright 2012 SEM Training LLC, 978-1-449-30838-4."

If you feel your use of examples or quotations from this book falls outside fair use or the permission given above, feel free to contact us at *permissions@oreilly.com*.

Safari® Books Online

 Safari Books Online is an on-demand digital library that lets you easily search over 7,500 technology and creative reference books and videos to find the answers you need quickly.

With a subscription, you can read any page and watch any video from our library online. Read books on your cell phone and mobile devices. Access new titles before they are available for print, and get exclusive access to manuscripts in development and post feedback for the authors. Copy and paste code samples, organize your favorites, download chapters, bookmark key sections, create notes, print out pages, and benefit from tons of other time-saving features.

O'Reilly Media has uploaded this book to the Safari Books Online service. To have full digital access to this book and others on similar topics from O'Reilly and other publishers, sign up for free at *http://my.safaribooksonline.com*.

How to Contact Us

Please address comments and questions concerning this book to the publisher:

O'Reilly Media, Inc.
1005 Gravenstein Highway North
Sebastopol, CA 95472
800-998-9938 (in the United States or Canada)
707-829-0515 (international or local)
707-829-0104 (fax)

We have a web page for this book, where we list errata, examples, and any additional information. You can access this page at:

http://shop.oreilly.com/product/0636920021124.do

To comment or ask technical questions about this book, send email to:

bookquestions@oreilly.com

For more information about our books, courses, conferences, and news, see our website at *http://www.oreilly.com*.

Find us on Facebook: *http://facebook.com/oreilly*

Follow us on Twitter: *http://twitter.com/oreillymedia*

Watch us on YouTube: *http://www.youtube.com/oreillymedia*

Acknowledgments

I would like to extend deep gratitude to the family, friends, and colleagues who made this book possible.

I owe a huge thanks to technical editors Heather Cooan and Mike Small.

Thanks to the all the Googlers I've worked with, especially Justin Cutroni, Betsy Schmitt, Helen Schindler, and Vivian Leung, for putting your faith in me at the start.

Thanks to David Booth, Corey Koberg, and the entire Cardinal Path team.

Thanks to my clients who put up with my absence and graciously allowed me to reference their accounts: Tom, Kent, Clive, Leslie, Julia, Tyler, David, and Peter. You are all wonderful!

Last but not least, a huge thanks to my incredibly supportive, patient, enviably charming, and attractive editors: Courtney Nash, Simon St. Laurent, and Teresa Elsey.

CHAPTER 1

Getting Started

Introduction to Google AdWords

AdWords is the name of Google's auction-based advertising platform. Launched in 2000, it evolved into a hotly contested marketplace for ad position on Google's search results pages. This chapter introduces basic AdWords concepts and how to create an account.

AdWords works because it doesn't seem like advertising. To Google's credit, the displayed advertising results are extremely relevant to the searcher's query. Ads are displayed at the moment someone is looking for something and presented as potential solutions to their search. This relevancy is the key to the effectiveness of the system for both searchers and advertisers.

Ads appear on Google.com (plus Google search with other country extensions: Google.ca (*http://goo.gl/c7uly*), Google.co.uk (*http://goo.gl/20H6H*), Google.fr (*http://goo.gl/reLnm*), etc.), other websites owned by Google, and websites that are members of Google's advertising network.

AdWords also displays ads on web pages and other places. In the case of websites that display AdWords ads, the ads are not triggered by a search on a keyword; they are contextually targeted to the content of the web page. A person reading movie reviews on Pajiba.com (*http://goo.gl/Exeo*) might see ads for upcoming movies, while a person reading the Business section of NYTimes.com (*http://goo.gl/UDlK1*) might see ads for insurance plans for employees. The most familiar ad format is the text ad, but image, Flash, video, and other interactive ad formats are available, too.

AdWords is not a "set it and forget it" platform. Campaigns should be regularly monitored, performance tracked and measured. A campaign that generated dozens of qualified leads last week may not perform well this week. The auction rules and user interface change frequently, a challenge for people unaccustomed to online software. That being said, a minimal commitment to managing an AdWords account can reap benefits. Like anything, the more you put in, the more you get back.

Where Ads Can Appear

Let's review how Google organizes search results. Google displays ads on *search results pages*, abbreviated SERPs (search engine results pages). To keep things interesting, SERPs change search-by-search; Google frequently changes formatting, colors, and layout of results pages. Figure 1-1 shows an example SERP.

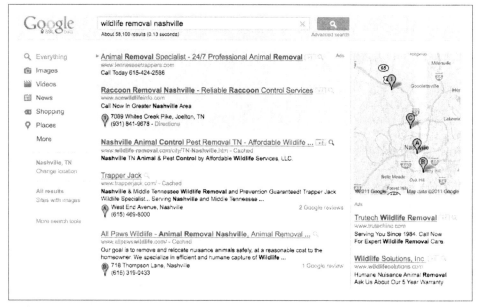

Figure 1-1. Google search engine results page (SERP)

A person went to Google.com (*http://goo.gl/LP38S*) and searched for `wildlife removal nashville`. This is called the *search query*. The search results page is created on the fly, displaying the most relevant results Google identifies for that particular searcher at that moment in time.

A single website can appear in multiple sections of the search results page, via AdWords or AdWords Express, Google Places, and the organic results. AdWords ads appear in the shaded box at the top of the page in the center section and the right column. Ads that appear in the shaded box are called *top-ranked ads*. This is a bonus given to advertisers whose keywords and ads closely match the search query, have a high click-through rate (CTR) on the ad and keyword, and meet a minimum bid threshold.

AdWords does not tell you what that threshold is; suffice it to say, aggressive bids are more likely to earn top-ranked positions. You cannot opt in or out of the top-ranked box; it's determined by algorithm. If no ads meet the quality and bid requirements for top-ranked placement, ads appear in the right column only.

If the shaded box does not appear on the SERP, the first AdWords ad appears in the right column. By default, there are up to 11 ads on a page. People can change this limit in their browser settings, but you should assume that the majority of searchers use the default.

Each business has a single opportunity to display an AdWords ad on a search results page—showing multiple ads for the same business, called double-serving, is not allowed. You are not charged when an ad displays (called an *impression*). Instead, you pay when searchers click the ad. This is why AdWords advertising is often described as *pay-per-click* (PPC) or a *cost-per-click* (CPC) model.

AdWords advertisers compete in a blind, instantaneous auction. The prize is ad placement, and the winners' ads show in higher positions on the search results page. So, a Nashville-based company specializing in the humane relocation of bats might choose to bid on the example keyword `wildlife removal nashville`, in an effort to display an ad to the searcher.

Back to the center column. Below the shaded box appears another set of search results, the coveted *organic* or *natural results*. These results are generated by a separate algorithm. Organic rank cannot be bought or influenced by advertising spending. Clicks on organic listings do not cost money, but it's a misnomer to call them free.

The process of optimizing these organic results is a separate online marketing strategy called *search engine optimization* (SEO), and many companies devote significant internal and external resources to it. If your website does not appear in the organic results, use AdWords—at least as an interim measure—to promote the website on key terms.

Search queries that include location-specific keywords often result in SERPs with an additional section labeled Places, shown in Figure 1-2. These results are labeled with a red eyedropper icon. Sometimes Places results are integrated with the organic results, displaying the pin icon with the website listing. These results have an associated Google Places page for the business.

Figure 1-2. Separate section for Google Places results

You may also notice AdWords ads labeled with a blue pin icon. This is a hybrid of AdWords and Google Places called AdWords Express (formerly known as Boost).

Google's search results pages vary, pulling results from other Google websites and products. To take advantage of these opportunities, online marketing strategies may include promotion via Google Merchant Center, YouTube, Google Images, blogs, and more.

Google's Networks

AdWords ads are not restricted to Google's SERPs. Google offers access to a huge advertising network with three major components: Search, the Search Partners, and the Google Display Network (GDN). These networks are referred to as *ad distribution preferences* in an AdWords account. As you see in Figure 1-3, ad distribution is managed in the Settings tab for each campaign. When creating a new campaign, it's important to note that all networks are enabled by default. Campaign settings are covered in Chapter 5.

Figure 1-3. Ad distribution preferences in campaign settings

Search includes Google.com and all other Google search domains (Google.ca (*http://goo.gl/JZatS*), Google.com.au (*http://goo.gl/kjouq*), Google.com.mx (*http://goo.gl/uYlFw*), etc.). Search supports text ads only.

The Search Partners, sometimes referred to as the Search Network, comprises a set of websites that use Google's algorithm for their internal site search function (often labeled "enhanced by Google"). Network membership changes from time to time. As of this writing, the network includes search partner websites like AOL.com (*http://goo.gl/ jGmvH*), plus Google Maps (*http://goo.gl/R0Twl*), Google Groups (*http://goo.gl/OK0eg*), Google Product Search (*http://www.google.com/prdhp*), and others. Figure 1-4 shows a few examples. Ads also appear on the mobile version of Google search: http://m.google.com (*http://goo.gl/M55q9*).

Figure 1-4. Search Partner examples

 On May 30, 2012, Google rolled out Google+ Local (*http://goo.gl/ 1GOHV*), which integrated business listings with the Google+ social platform. Places pages were automatically migrated into the Google+ Local format. It's assumed that at some point Google Places will be entirely replaced with Google+ Local.

To show ads on the Search Partners, a campaign must also be opted into Google Search. The Search Partners is an all-or-nothing network, so you cannot include or exclude particular websites. From a competition perspective, the Search Partners network operates the same way as Google Search. A person must complete a search on a network website; the AdWords auction determines which ads display, based on keywords selected by advertisers. The only difference is that individual sites may change the visual presentation of the text ads. These ads typically display with two or four lines.

The third network, the Google Display Network (GDN), is very different from Search and the Search Partners. This network consists primarily of websites opted into Google's AdSense program.

AdSense allows website publishers to show ads on web pages in exchange for a percentage of the profit when visitors click the ads. The network includes millions of website, video, gaming, and mobile partners that display AdWords ads. The network also includes YouTube, Blogger, Gmail, and other Google properties.

The places where ads appear are collectively referred to as *placements*. In your AdWords account, *automatic placements* refer to placements selected by AdWords to display ads. *Managed placements* refer to placements you manually select to display ads. You have the option to exclude placements, including entire domains, subdirectories, or individual pages within a site.

So how is the GDN different? It's simple: there wasn't a search. The person who sees your ad happened to visit a web page that shows AdWords ads, with a topic *related* to your keywords. As you see in Figure 1-5, a person visiting the Angry Birds fan site, AngryBirdsNest.com (*http://goo.gl/gRc1F*), might see an image ad for the Wii game Go Vacation (*http://goo.gl/l05We*). This ad is labeled "Ads by Google."

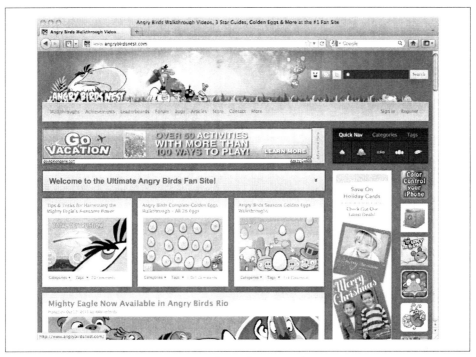

Figure 1-5. A Google image ad, via the Google Display Network

If you're just starting with AdWords, it's a good idea to turn the Google Display Network off because it is so different from search and requires separate strategy and optimization techniques. Chapter 9 covers advertising on the Display Network.

Creating a Google Account

Before using Google's products, you are required to set up a Google account. This account operates as a universal login for all associated Google products. Having one login makes things simple because you won't need separate usernames and passwords for AdWords, Gmail, Google Places, Google Analytics, etc. You can register an existing email address as a Google account; a Gmail account is already a Google account.

Google accounts are free and take about one minute to set up (assuming you can figure out the CAPTCHA, it takes me several tries). Figure 1-6 shows the registration form.

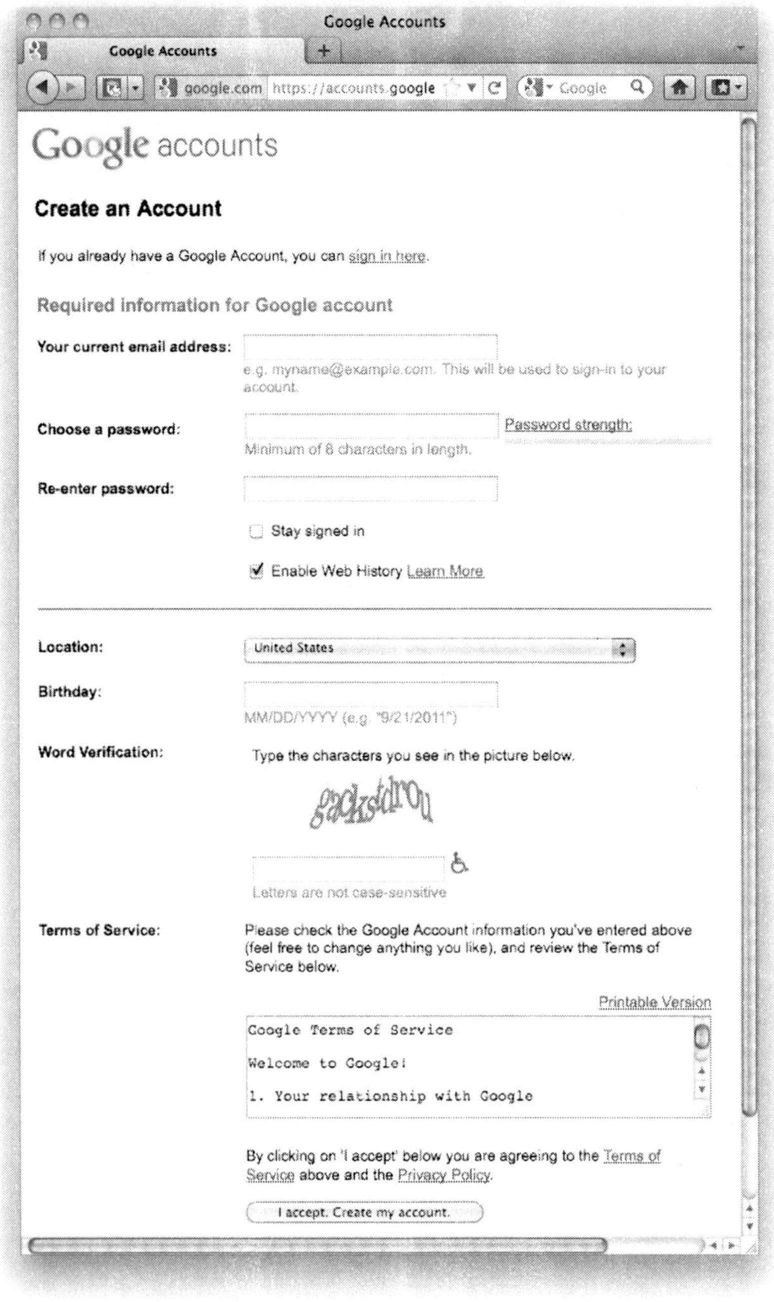

Figure 1-6. Start by creating a Google account

You must provide:

- Your email address
- Password
- Location (country)
- Your birth date
- Word verification (CAPTCHA)
- Acceptance of Google's Terms of Service

To create a Google account, visit www.google.com/accounts (*http://goo.gl/ZXMM1*).

 One common issue people experience is difficulty connecting Google products associated with different Google accounts (for example, connecting a Google Analytics account to an AdWords account). It's best to use the same Google account for all Google products used by your company. In this scenario, use the same username and password to login to AdWords, Google Places, Google Merchant Center, Google Analytics, and so on.

Creating an AdWords Account

Once you have a Google account, it's time to set up an AdWords account at www.google.com/adwords (*http://goo.gl/n6Wr2*).

Figure 1-7 shows the sign in/sign up screen. Click the "Start now" button.

 Alternatively, call (877) 721-1738 Monday–Friday 9 a.m.–9 p.m. ET for help creating an account.

You already created a Google Account, so select the radio button that says "I have an email address and password I already use with Google services like AdSense, Gmail, Orkut, or iGoogle."

Now, select the radio button that says "I'd like to use my existing Google account for AdWords" and login with your username and password.

Now you will select your billing country from the drop-down menu and click Continue. Next, enter your billing profile information, associated with your payment method, then click Continue.

Finally, agree to the terms and conditions and the AdWords account is officially activated. The new account is identified by the *customer ID* (CID), a ten-digit number formatted like a phone number, in the top right corner of the page. Occasionally a new

Figure 1-7. Click the red "Start Now" button at the top right corner to create an AdWords account

account does not display the customer ID immediately; it should appear within 24 hours. Use this number to identify your account in any correspondence with Google.

Managing Account Access

When creating an AdWords account, you must provide a primary login email address. This email address cannot be changed or removed from the account. An email address is associated with a single AdWords account.

 Set up a company email address or Gmail account specifically for Ad-Words and other Google products (for example, *google@mycompany.com* or *mycompany@gmail.com*). Use this login for all the Google products associated with the company. Do not use an employee's personal email address; if she leaves the company, you will have access headaches because Google products cannot be transferred to other accounts.

You can create multiple logins for the same AdWords account and assign various access permissions. The access levels are as follows:

Administrative access
> Can view, edit, and manage any part of the account. Can invite other users, change access levels, and disable access.

Standard access and Standard (managed) access
> Can view, edit, and manage any part of the account. Cannot invite others, change access levels, or disable access.

Read only access and Read only (managed) access
> Can view the Campaigns and Opportunities tabs in read-only mode, as well as view and run reports.

Email only access
> Cannot access the account but can receive account reports and other notifications via email.

An email address cannot be associated with more than one AdWords account. If you need to access multiple accounts, create multiple Google Accounts, one for each Ad-Words account.

Setting Up Your First Campaign

The first time you login to AdWords, you may see the splash screen similar to Figure 1-8. Some new accounts skip this splash screen and lead straight to the Campaigns tab.

Click "Create your first campaign" to initiate a campaign creation wizard. You can launch a campaign in a matter of minutes (but don't set this campaign live until you have an understanding of how settings, keywords, bids, and creative impact performance). Let's look at the basic steps to create a campaign.

1. The wizard starts with campaign settings, including campaign name, target location and language, and bids. Chapter 5 covers campaign settings in detail.

2. Next, write an ad, select keywords and placements, and set bids. Chapter 6 covers keywords, Chapter 7 covers writing ads, and Chapter 11 covers bidding models.

3. Save changes by clicking the "Save and continue to billing" button or "Set up billing later." If you choose the latter, the campaign is saved, but ads do not run until billing information is added. Billing options are explained in Chapter 11.

And that's it! Setting up the campaign literally takes one minute, but there's no telling if it was set up well. This wizard walks you through a single campaign and ad group, with little explanation about the settings you selected or the effectiveness of the ads, keywords, and bids.

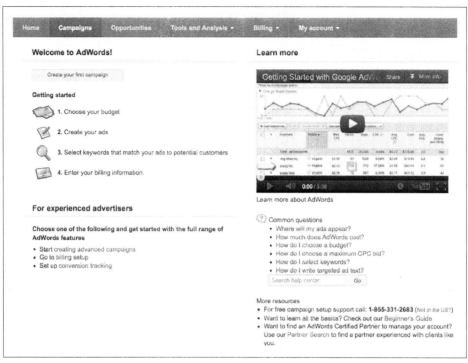

Figure 1-8. The AdWords new account splash screen

Now that the campaign framework is created, additional work is required to ensure that you set the account up for success. The following chapters explain how to navigate the account and implement strategies to make sure ad dollars are well spent.

If you'd like to optimize the campaign before spending money, change the status to Paused until you're ready to go live.

CHAPTER 2

Understanding the Auction

How the AdWords Auction Works

Before discussing account optimization, it's helpful to understand how AdWords works. AdWords is an auction, conducted in real-time every time a person completes a search. Auction winners have their ads displayed on the top and right side of the Google search results page. The highest-placing winners achieve more prominent ad positions on the page, relative to other advertisers.

The auction calculations happen in milliseconds; searchers have no idea that AdWords has sorted through millions of keywords to determine which ads appear on the page. Here's how it works:

When someone searches on Google, AdWords compares the search query to every keyword in advertisers' accounts, identifying keywords that match or are closely related to the query. Each match represents an entry in the auction and an advertiser who wants to display an ad on the search results page.

AdWords then generates a real-time Quality Score for each keyword to determine which have sufficient quality to participate in the auction. The algorithm considers many factors, including the keyword's clickthrough rate, the relevancy of the ad text and search query, and the quality of the landing page. If the keyword's Quality Score is too low, AdWords will not display the ad, no matter how much the advertiser is willing to pay.

Once AdWords identifies keywords with passable Quality Scores, the auction resumes. Now, AdWords calculates Quality Score a second time. This calculation is similar to the first, except it does not factor in landing page quality. AdWords multiplies this second score and the keyword's Max CPC bid to calculate a rank. The highest ranking keyword wins first place in the auction, and the corresponding ad is displayed in the first ad position on Google's search results page. Ads for keywords with lower rank are displayed in descending order.

On October 3, 2011, Inside AdWords (*http://goo.gl/wK5K8*) announced an "ads quality improvement" change that increases the weight given to relevance and landing page quality in determining Quality Score and how ads are ranked. The changes apply only to ads on Google Search and do not affect ads on Search Partners or on the Google Display Network. If you ran AdWords campaigns prior to that date, monitor keyword Quality Score and average ad position.

Previously, Ad Rank was calculated using the following formula:

```
Ad Rank = (Quality Score) × (Max CPC bid)
```

Now, Ad Rank is described as "a combination of Max CPC bid and Quality Score."

The new formula looks like:

```
Ad Rank = f(Quality Score, Max CPC bid)
```

Bids are a big factor in the AdWords auction. However, you cannot simply buy a position on the page; Quality Score ensures that ads are relevant to the search query. It also serves to level the playing field for advertisers with limited budgets who compete against retail giants with significant resources. In some cases, it's possible to win a higher position in the auction with a lower bid.

The amount paid for a click, called the *actual cost per click*, is determined by a formula called the AdWords Discounter. The Maximum CPC bid indicates the *most* you will pay for a click, but the actual CPC is often lower. Here's how it works:

```
Ad Rank of Competitor Below You ÷ Your Quality Score + 1 cent = Actual Cost Per Click
```

Consider this scenario. You won the AdWords auction. Your keyword has a Max CPC bid of $.75 and a Quality Score of 9. The advertiser in second place has an Ad Rank of 6.25. The formula to calculate your actual cost per click looks like this:

```
6.25 ÷ 9 + .01 = $.70
```

So, even though your Max CPC bid is $.75, you pay $.70 for the top ad position. The formula is applied to all advertisers. For the advertiser in second place, the formula might look like this:

```
4 (Ad Rank of third-place advertiser) ÷ 5 (Advertiser #2's Quality Score) + .01 = $.81
```

The advertiser in second place pays $.11 more than the auction winner! If the third-place advertiser does not have any ads below him in the auction, he pays a minimum price to appear on the search results page, a price determined by AdWords that cannot be seen in the account.

What Is Quality Score?

Quality Score is one of the most important numbers in your AdWords account. Google generally defines it as a measurement of the usefulness of your ads to the searcher, but there's a lot more to it. Quality Score is a dynamically generated variable; every single time a search query matches one of your keywords, AdWords recalculates Quality Score.

There are various Quality Scores associated with an account, but from an advertiser perspective, the only one you see is keyword Quality Score. This score is not displayed by default, so start by enabling the column from the Keywords roll-up tab. Once it's enabled, you see Quality Score displayed as a whole number from 1 to 10. The higher the Quality Score, the better. As a general rule of thumb, a range of 1–4 is poor, 5–7 is OK, and 8–10 is great.

The number you see in your account represents the general quality of your keyword when exactly matching a search on Google. Let's say a keyword ran for year with an average Quality Score of 2. In the last month you significantly improved the performance of the keyword, bringing the new average Quality Score to 8. AdWords won't penalize you for a year of poor performance; instead it displays the new average score so you get a better picture of how you currently compete in the auction.

Why Does Quality Matter?

Quality Score impacts three important outcomes in the AdWords auction:

- Quality Score determines whether your keyword is eligible to compete in the Ad-Words auction.
- If the keyword is eligible, Quality Score is part of the calculation used to determine who wins the auction. Winners are ranked; this ranking system determines where ads appear on the page in relation to each other.
- If an ad wins a place on the page, Quality Score affects the actual amount you pay for the click.

Quality Score is also used to calculate first page bid estimates, an optional column visible under the Keywords roll-up tab. This metric ballparks the Max CPC bid required, per keyword, to show an ad on the first page of Google's search results. This estimate is based on the keyword's Quality Score and current advertiser competition. My experience is that this estimate is often high, and ads usually display at a lower price. However, a high estimate is a red flag that the keyword's Quality Score needs improvement.

Here's how Quality Score factors into the auction on Google Search and the Search Partners: when a Google search matches one of your keywords, the AdWords system calculates the keyword's Quality Score. This calculation determines whether the quality is high enough to participate in the AdWords auction.

If the keyword's Quality Score is too low, the ad cannot be displayed, no matter how high the bid. You might be the only advertiser competing for the keyword, but if the keyword Quality Score is too low, AdWords will not show your ad.

If the keyword passes this initial test, it enters the AdWords auction, along with all other keywords that passed. Quality Score is calculated again; this score is part of the calculation that determines ad rank and the winners of the auction.

How Is Quality Score Calculated?

AdWords uses a variety of factors to determine the Quality Score for a keyword. You can improve some; others are out of your control. Google does not specify precise weightings of the factors, because the Quality Score models are complex, dynamic, and dependent on each unique advertisers' specific performance history for each query.

For ads appearing on Google search results pages, AdWords considers the following factors:

Clickthrough rate (CTR)
> This is the most important factor used to determine Quality Score—the higher the CTR, the better. AdWords rewards ads and keywords that receive more clicks. A click is an indication that the ad and keyword are compelling and relevant (and clicks are how Google makes money). Think of each click as a vote for the ad and corresponding keyword.

Ad relevancy
> AdWords compares the relevancy of the keyword to the ad text in the ad group. The more closely they match, the better. Relevancy tends to improve CTR as well. If a searcher wants to find `organic dog rawhides` and this phrase is the headline of the ad, the ad has a good chance of getting the click.

Search query relevancy
> AdWords compares the search query to the keyword and matched ad.

AdWords account history
> This is measured by the CTR of all ads and keywords in the account.

Display URLs
> AdWords considers the historical CTR of display URLs in the ad group.

Landing page quality
> This factor is considered in the first calculation only, to determine if a keyword can participate in the auction. It does not factor into the ad rank equation.

Geographic performance
> The account's performance in the geographic area where the ads are displayed is considered.

Other relevance factors
> Quality Score is also influenced by additional factors AdWords won't tell us about.

The Quality Score used to calculate first page bid estimates is based on the same factors, except it does not consider the ad relevancy or search query relevancy.

For the Search Partners, Quality Score is based on the same factors, except:

Clickthrough rate (CTR)
> AdWords considers CTR for that particular site, in addition to CTR across the entire Search Network.

For the Google Display Network with automatic placements, Quality Score is based on the following factors:

Past performance
> The ad's past performance on this website and similar sites.

Relevancy
> The relevance of the ads and keywords to the website.

Landing page quality

Other relevance factors
> Additional factors AdWords won't tell us about.

For targeted placements on the Google Display Network with cost-per-click bidding, Quality Score is based on the following factors:

Clickthrough rate (CTR)
> The historical CTR of the ad on this website and similar sites.

Landing page quality

For ads appearing on targeted placements on the Google Display Network with CPM bidding, Quality Score is based on only one factor: landing page quality.

Where to Find Quality Score

There are three ways to see Quality Score for keywords in your AdWords account. Start by clicking the Campaigns tab. Then select the part of the account you want to review from the tree view: "All online campaigns," a campaign, or an ad group. Now, select the Keywords tab from the roll-up tabs in the middle pane. Keywords appear in rows, with columns of associated data.

In the Status column, you see if the keyword is active; click the small thought bubble icon (💬) to see Quality Score in the box (see Figure 2-1). When you click this icon, you see several important pieces of information: first, if ads are showing. For this example keyword, "unique wedding bands for men," ads are running and the keyword has a perfect Quality Score, 10 out of 10.

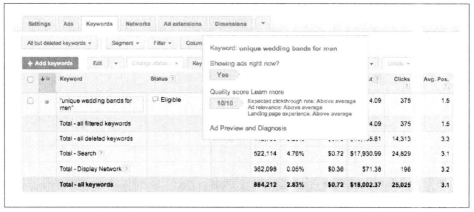

Figure 2-1. View Quality Score from the status column

The status column option is great because it tells us if ads are running. If the ad group has hundreds of keywords, it's inefficient to click each keyword's Status column to review Quality Score. An easy fix: enable the Quality Score column, which is curiously off by default. To do this, click the Columns button and then "Customize columns" from the drop-down menu (see Figure 2-2). A list of optional columns appears. From the Attributes section, click "Add" next to Qual. score, then click Save. The Quality Score column appears in the middle pane view, with each keyword.

Click the "Qual. score" column header to arrange keywords high-to-low or low-to-high.

Figure 2-2. Enable the Quality Score column

A third option for viewing Quality Score is using filters. Let's say you want to review keywords with extremely high scores. Create a filter to show keywords that have a

Quality Score greater than or equal to 9 (see Figure 2-3). You can use this filter whether you enabled the Quality Score column or not; the filter shows all keywords that match your criteria.

Figure 2-3. Filter by Quality Score

There is one additional place to see keyword Quality Score, not in the AdWords account user interface but in AdWords Editor (see Figure 2-4). Open the AdWords account in the editor and navigate to the Keywords tab. As in the online user interface, you see columns with each keyword row. If Quality Score is not visible, turn it on by clicking the icon at the top right corner of the column headings and clicking Quality Score from the drop-down menu.

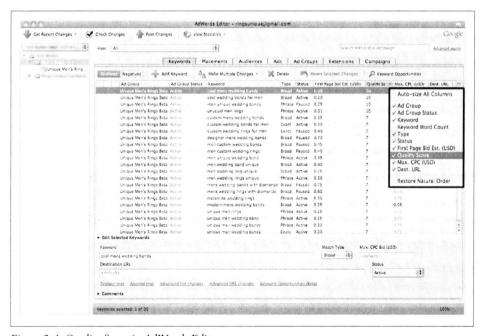

Figure 2-4. Quality Score in AdWords Editor

Ad Position, CTR, and Quality Score

Ads with higher rank show in higher positions on Google's search results page, often in the yellow box above the organic search results. Top-ranked ads typically receive more clicks than ads appearing lower on the page. This being the case, you may worry that a lower position with a lower CTR hurts the Quality Score of associated keywords. AdWords actually accounts for this difference.

To determine Quality Score, AdWords compares the CTR to ads displayed *in the same position*. So, the CTR of an ad showing at the bottom of the search results page is not compared to the CTR for a top-ranked ad.

How to Improve Quality Score

Improving Quality Score is occasionally a frustrating exercise, but in most cases, a few simple tweaks will improve scores. Optimizing for Quality Score boils down to two primary objectives: improving CTR and increasing relevancy.

First, identify keywords with low Quality Score. Do this in any of the ways described above; I like to use filters to isolate poor performers. Start by displaying all keywords with a Quality Score of less than or equal to four. Low Quality Scores bring down overall ad group quality, so some action should be taken on these keywords. The simplest solution is to pause or delete them. But some of the keywords may be relevant to the advertised business, and deleting them sacrifices important impressions. What to do?

Start by reviewing CTR. Low-quality keywords often have low CTR, which means the ad was displayed, but searchers did not click. Good CTR varies by keyword. A generic keyword might be doing well to hit 1 percent. A more specific, long-tail keyword might hit double-digit CTR. Click the CTR column header to sort. Once you identify low-quality keywords with poor CTR, the challenge is to figure out why. Possible reasons include the following:

- The displayed ad was not relevant to the searcher's query.
- The displayed ad was relevant, but not compelling.

So, how do you fix the problem? For this example, let's use the keyword organic rawhide dog chews. It has a Quality Score of three and a CTR of .02 percent. Start by looking at the ads associated with the ad group. Your ad might read something like this:

```
Pet Supply Store
All natural products for dogs,
cats, fish, rodents and more.
example.com
```

Notice that the ad is not specific to the associated keyword. It mentions dogs, but it makes no reference to organic rawhide chews. AdWords is an algorithm, and as such, very literal. The ad itself is uninspired—nothing sets it apart, it has no specific theme or offer, and it lacks a call to action. A better ad would incorporate the keyword in the text of the ad, preferably as the headline and/or the Display URL. Some of the keywords might appear in the Description lines (just take care that the ad isn't too repetitive):

```
Organic Rawhide Dog Chews
Make Dogs Happy & Clean Their Teeth
Many Flavors Available, Order Now!
example.com/Organic-Dog-Rawhides
```

This ad is focused on the keyword, improving Quality Score from a relevancy perspective. This approach usually improves CTR, because searchers tend to click well-written ads that prominently feature the search query.

Now the ad is specific to the keyword, but does it represent *all* the keywords in the ad group? Take a look at the keywords in the list. If all keywords are closely related to organic rawhide dog chews, the ad should be relevant for the entire group. But what if the ad group includes other keywords that do not match as closely? For example, the keyword list might include Greenies, a type of dog chew. But Greenies are not organic or rawhide, and the word "Greenies" does not appear in the ad text. What if the ad group includes the word Kong or dog de-shedding tool?

If you find keywords in the ad group that do not fit the central theme, the account needs reorganization. In this case, you might create new ad groups for Greenies, Kong, and dog de-shedding. Then, write ads specific to these themes and move the appropriate keywords to their new ad groups.

Now the keyword is relevant to the ad text, but what about the relevancy to the search query? Chapter 6 covers keyword match types in detail. In the meantime, know that a keyword's match type determines how closely the search query must match to trigger an ad. If your keywords are all broad match, the default, AdWords has tremendous leeway to determine which queries match keywords. For example, if your keyword is organic dog chews, AdWords could inadvertently show your ad for search queries like these:

- chew proof dog bed
- why do dogs chew their feet
- dog muzzles for chewing
- organic chewing gum

In this case, your ad may be shown on search queries that are unrelated to the theme of the ad group. A searcher wants organic chewing gum, and she sees your ad for organic dog chews!

To correct the issue, you must prevent ads from showing on unrelated queries. There are two ways to accomplish this: make keyword match types more restrictive or build a negative keyword list to filter irrelevant search queries. Chapter 6 covers the pros and cons of each approach.

For the purposes of the Quality Score discussion, the point is that you don't want your ad to show when searchers are looking for something else. Searchers will probably skip your ad, which hurts CTR. If they *do* click your ad, it helps CTR but probably not your business, since the searchers were looking for another type of product.

CHAPTER 3

Account Structure

How AdWords Accounts Are Organized

This chapter explains AdWords account structure and illustrates how important structure is to the success of your campaigns. All AdWords accounts are organized on three levels: account, campaign, and ad group, shown in Figure 3-1.

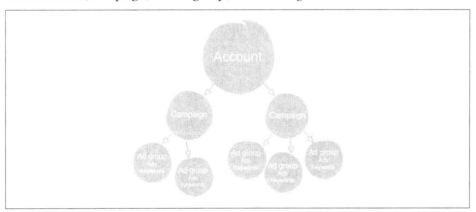

Figure 3-1. AdWords account structure

After you create an AdWords account, a setup wizard walks you through the first campaign and ad group. Going forward, it's important to understand the difference between them. Campaigns control settings, including the daily budget, the networks where ads display, geographic targets, and the like. Chapter 5 explains campaign settings in detail.

Ad groups fall within campaigns, and the campaign settings apply to all ad groups within a campaign. Ad groups contain the ads, keywords, and they designate the maximum amount you are willing to pay for a click (the max CPC bid). To recap:

Account level
    Controls administrative information, such as account access and billing.

Campaign level

Campaigns specify settings that apply to all ad groups within them.

Ad group level

Ad groups contain keywords, ads, websites (placements) that ads appear on, and bids (the maximum you're willing to pay for an ad click).

Default account limits are as follows:

- 10,000 campaigns (this includes active and paused campaigns)
- 20,000 ad groups per campaign
- 5,000 keywords per ad group (this includes negative keywords)
- 300 display ads per ad group (this includes image ads)
- 4 million ads per account (this includes active and paused ads)
- 5 million keywords per account
- 10,000 location targets per campaign
- 100,000 active ad extensions per account
- 1.3 million references to ad extensions per account

Why Structure Matters

Lack of structure is the most common issue with an AdWords account. If you understand and implement proper account structure, you will have an enormous advantage over competitors who don't.

Poorly structured accounts are easily recognized, because they usually contain a single campaign with a single ad group. The ad group may contain hundreds of keywords that describe many aspects of the advertised products and services.

Successful AdWords accounts typically contain many ad groups, each focused on a single theme. Each ad group contains keywords and ad text relevant to the chosen theme.

Imagine this scenario: an advertiser uses AdWords to promote a nursery that sells plants and gardening supplies. The AdWords account has a single campaign and ad group, and the keyword list includes 2,000 keywords, ranging from the name of the nursery to Latin names of plants it sells. A sample of the keyword list might look like this:

- jasmine's nursery
- buy lavender plants
- thornless blackberry bushes
- beekeeping supplies
- tumbling compost bins

- organic black krim tomatoes
- lavandula x intermedia grosso

The ad group includes one text ad:

```
Jasmine's Nursery
We Sell What Organic Gardens Need.
Plants, Seeds & Supplies - Buy Now!
example.com
```

Now, imagine a searcher on Google, looking for beekeeping equipment. His search query, `beekeeping supplies`, triggers an ad based on this keyword list. But the corresponding ad is generic, and the searcher might pass it by without clicking to learn more. To improve performance, the advertiser creates many ad groups, each focused on a single theme. The seven keyword examples might become the themes for seven separate ad groups. This structure allows relevant ads to display, based on the theme of the ad group.

Once a theme is defined, additional related keywords are added to each ad group. For example, the ad group focused on beekeeping supplies might contain keywords like:

- beekeepers veil
- bee keeper helmet
- tulle veil for beekeeping
- beekeeper suit
- leather bee gloves

Now, when the searcher sees the ad, it could read:

```
Beekeeper Equipment
We Sell Everything Your Bees Need.
Bee Suits, Veils & More. Buy Now!
example.com
```

An ad click should not send the searcher to the nursery's homepage; instead it should land on the beekeeping section. Now it's up to the website to make the purchase process simple. If the searcher buys the veil—and maybe a matching pith helmet—the ad click resulted in a sale, and success for the advertiser.

In theory, each keyword can be a separate ad group with corresponding ad text and a destination URL. So, if someone searches for `tulle veil for beekeeping`, the ad text reads "Tulle Veil for Beekeeping" instead of "Beekeeper Equipment." An ad click sends the searcher directly to the product page for the tulle veil, rather than the page with all beekeeper products.

If your AdWords account has hundreds or thousands of keywords, this approach is impractical, but you can apply the strategy to the most popular and profitable keywords.

Your Organization Strategy

There is no one right way to organize an AdWords account. When creating campaigns, review the settings to see if you need more than one campaign. For example, if you plan to run ads in English and Spanish, you need two campaigns, each targeting a single language. If you want to display some ads in the United States and other ads in Canada, you need separate campaigns with different geotargets. Chapter 5 covers campaign settings in detail. You may determine that a single campaign is sufficient.

Ad groups are a different story. Successful AdWords accounts typically include many ad groups, each focused on a single theme. Here are some ideas for developing and organizing ad groups within campaigns:

- Products
- Services
- Themes
- Your website structure
- Websites (one domain name per ad group)
- Brands
- Seasons
- Holidays
- Problems to solve
- Symptoms of problems
- Synonyms
- Misspellings

Review the settings for your existing campaign. If you'd like to apply different settings to the new ad groups, create a new campaign. If all settings will remain the same, create an ad group within that campaign. If you prefer to keep the new ad groups separate, create a new campaign with duplicate settings. Remember, each new campaign requires a daily budget, which increases total potential ad spending. AdWords does not have an account-level budget cap, so your total budget is the sum of all campaign daily budgets.

Campaign or ad group?

Here's a typical scenario: an advertiser wants to use AdWords to promote a new product or service. He's unsure whether he should create a new campaign or a new ad group. To determine the best approach, consider the following questions:

Do the new ads require a separate budget?
> If yes, create a new campaign with its own daily budget. To roll new ads into an existing budget, create ad groups within that campaign.

Do you want to use a different bidding model for the new ads?
     If yes, create a new campaign. If not, create an ad group within that campaign.
Do the new ads target a different geographic area?
     If yes, create a new campaign. If not, create an ad group within that campaign.
Are the new ads written in a different language?
     If yes, create a new campaign. If not, create an ad group within that campaign.
     Google does not translate keywords or ads.
Do the new ads target different networks or devices?
     If yes, create a new campaign. If not, create an ad group within that campaign.

Another common question is how many keywords should be included in each ad group. Google often recommends small numbers of keywords (five to 20). Rather than focusing on specific number, think of as many ways a searcher might try to find your business. Then, consider the theme of the ad group and review the keywords. If at any point, the themes of the keywords diverge, split them into different ad groups. Some ad groups may have just a few keywords; others may have thousands. Chapter 6 covers keywords,

Develop an AdWords strategy focused on your online objectives. Here are some ideas to get started.

Service Providers

For this example, let's set up a campaign for an irrigation company offering services in Burlington, Massachusetts, USA (see Figure 3-2). This company offers design, installation, and service, so each theme becomes an ad group. Set separate bids for each ad group, if desired. Service is this company's most profitable area, so the bid is set higher for that ad group. Notice the settings at the campaign level, and then notice how ad groups within focus on a single theme.

If the company wants to advertise in more areas, it could add additional locations to the existing campaign. But what if the company wants to use different settings for different areas—say, different budgets? In that case, it would create new campaigns within the account. Notice the difference in Figure 3-3; the new campaign has an identical structure, but the campaign settings target Amherst, not Burlington. The new campaign has its own daily budget: $25/day. Remember that this impacts total ad spending: the advertiser's new budget is $40/day (Campaign #1 @ $15 + Campaign #2 @ $25).

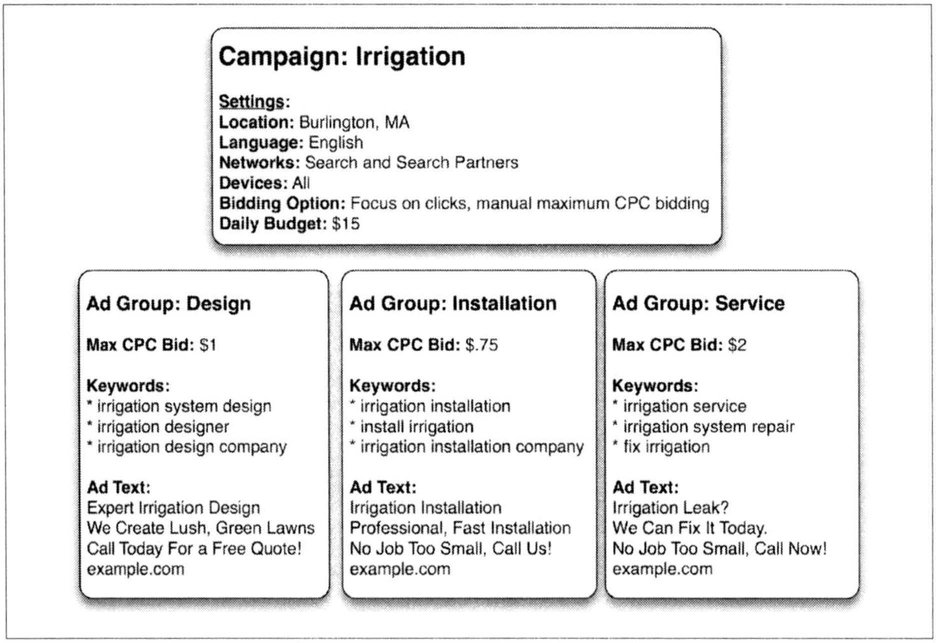

Campaign: Irrigation

Settings:
Location: Burlington, MA
Language: English
Networks: Search and Search Partners
Devices: All
Bidding Option: Focus on clicks, manual maximum CPC bidding
Daily Budget: $15

Ad Group: Design

Max CPC Bid: $1

Keywords:
* irrigation system design
* irrigation designer
* irrigation design company

Ad Text:
Expert Irrigation Design
We Create Lush, Green Lawns
Call Today For a Free Quote!
example.com

Ad Group: Installation

Max CPC Bid: $.75

Keywords:
* irrigation installation
* install irrigation
* irrigation installation company

Ad Text:
Irrigation Installation
Professional, Fast Installation
No Job Too Small, Call Us!
example.com

Ad Group: Service

Max CPC Bid: $2

Keywords:
* irrigation service
* irrigation system repair
* fix irrigation

Ad Text:
Irrigation Leak?
We Can Fix It Today.
No Job Too Small, Call Now!
example.com

Figure 3-2. Campaign for a service provider

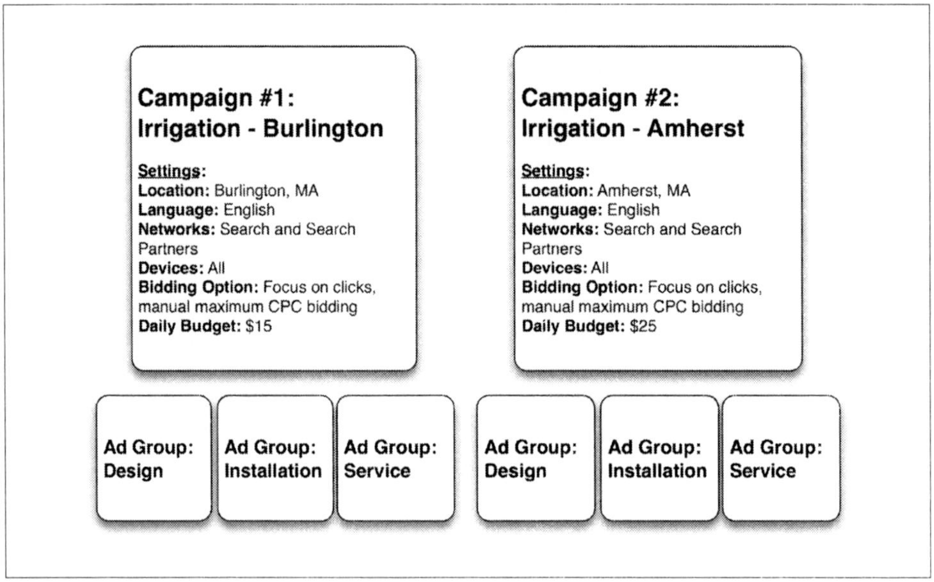

**Campaign #1:
Irrigation - Burlington**

Settings:
Location: Burlington, MA
Language: English
Networks: Search and Search
Partners
Devices: All
Bidding Option: Focus on clicks,
manual maximum CPC bidding
Daily Budget: $15

**Campaign #2:
Irrigation - Amherst**

Settings:
Location: Amherst, MA
Language: English
Networks: Search and Search
Partners
Devices: All
Bidding Option: Focus on clicks,
manual maximum CPC bidding
Daily Budget: $25

**Ad Group:
Design**

**Ad Group:
Installation**

**Ad Group:
Service**

**Ad Group:
Design**

**Ad Group:
Installation**

**Ad Group:
Service**

Figure 3-3. Multiple campaigns for a service provider

This service provider could also structure ad groups by the problems or symptoms being searched for or the desired outcome: help dying plants, grass turning yellow, make my grass green.

Brick and Mortar—Non-Ecommerce

For this example, let's create a campaign for a high-end pet supply store with a brick and mortar store in Buffalo, New York, USA (see Figure 3-4). There are many ways this company could organize the account. Ad groups might include:

Types of animals
> Dogs, cats, birds; or more specific (senior dogs, puppies, kittens); or breed specific (German shepherds, Siamese cats)

Types of food
> Kibble, canned food, treats, chews

Product brands
> Orijen, Greenies, PureVita, Nutro, Canidae, Felidae

Special dietary needs
> Grain-free dog food, corn-based dog food formula, dog food for sensitive stomach, cat food hairball formula

Training needs
> Martingale collar, electric dog fence, dog crate, agility equipment

Problems to solve
> Chewing, spraying, house training, escaping, aggression

Branding/local awareness
> Helping locals find the store

One of their campaigns might look like Figure 3-4.

Campaign: Dogs

Settings:
Location: Buffalo, NY
Language: English
Networks: All
Devices: All
Bidding Option: Focus on clicks, automatic bidding, no CPC bid limit
Daily Budget: $10

Ad Group: General Dog Food	**Ad Group: Senior Dog Food**	**Ad Group: Puppy Food**
Max CPC Bid: $1	**Max CPC Bid:** $1.50	**Max CPC Bid:** $1.50
Keywords: * all-natural dog food * organic dog food * specialty dog food	**Keywords:** * senior dog food * food for elderly dog * help old dog lose weight	**Keywords:** * premium puppy food * diet for puppies * organic puppy kibble
Ad Text: Premium Dog Food Buffalo's Premier Pet Supply Store Open 7 Days, Come In and See Us! example.com	**Ad Text:** Senior Dog Diet Great Selection and Prices. Open 7 Days, Come In and See Us! example.com	**Ad Text:** Champion-Grade Puppy Food Buffalo's Premier Pet Supply Store Open 7 Days, Come In and See Us! example.com

Figure 3-4. Campaign for a brick and mortar store

Ecommerce

If the goal of your AdWords campaign is *direct response* —when a click results in an immediate conversion— you may have the greatest success using specific keywords, especially those that indicate purchase intent. For this example, let's create a campaign for an ecommerce website selling rare and out-of-print books (see Figure 3-5). The campaign controls the settings; ad group ideas include the following:

- Product names (book titles)
- Product attributes (authors, publishers, first editions, signed books, etc.)
- Product model numbers (ISBN)

One of the campaigns might look like Figure 3-5.

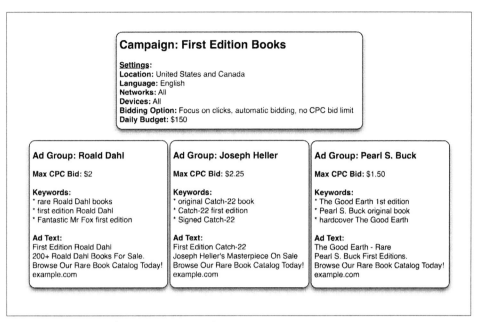

Figure 3-5. Campaign for an ecommerce website

Common Pitfalls

There are several account structure pitfalls. Let's look at them, and how to fix them.

Pitfall 1: Duplicate Keywords

When an account has identical duplicate keywords across competing campaigns and ad groups, the duplicates compete against each other. Only one ads per business can appear on a search results page. Every time someone searches with Google, the AdWords system identifies advertisers who want to display ads for that query. Each advertiser is entered into an auction, and the winners' ads are displayed on the search results page. Entering the AdWords auction multiple times creates the following problems:

1. Identical duplicate keywords bid against each other, possibly raising the actual cost for the click.

2. Identical duplicate keywords associated with different campaigns and ad groups compete, but only one ad can display. The winner may not be the preferred ad for the search query.

How to fix the problem: The easiest way to identify duplicate keywords is using the AdWords Editor tool. This standalone application can be downloaded by visiting www.google.com/adwordseditor (*http://goo.gl/NBTdX*). AdWords Editor includes a Tools section with a Find Duplicate Keywords feature. This tool quickly identifies duplicates across the account, across campaigns, and across ad groups.

Pitfall 2: Competing, Non-Duplicate Keywords

A trickier problem to correct is when similar keywords compete against each other for placement in the AdWords auction. These keywords do not bid against each other; rather, they compete for the opportunity to participate in the AdWords auction. This becomes a problem if you want to associate a specific ad and landing page with a theme but AdWords chooses another!

Let's say you advertise for a company offering HVAC installation and repair. The campaign has three ad groups based on the themes HVAC, air conditioners, and heating units. The keywords in each ad group relate to the themes, but they are all *broad match*. Broad match keywords can trigger ads when the search query is similar (see "Keyword Match Types" on page 88). So what happens if the search query is `repair heat and air unit`? Which ad group will AdWords choose? It's possible that AdWords considers all three ad groups relevant; only one will enter the auction.

To control which ads are served for particular search queries, decide upfront which ad groups best fit keyword variations. Then, use negative keywords (see "Negative Keywords" on page 91) to funnel variations to the appropriate ad group. Table 3-1 shows how it might look.

Table 3-1. Using negative keywords with ad groups

Ad Group: HVAC	Ad Group: Air Conditioner	Ad Group: Heating
Keywords:	Keywords:	Keywords:
• HVAC installation	• air conditioning installation	• heating unit
• HVAC units	• air conditioner installation	• heater installation
• HVAC companies	• AC installation	• heat installation
Negative Keywords:	Negative Keywords:	Negative Keywords:
• -"air conditioner"	• -HVAC	• -HVAC
• -heating	• -heating	• -"air conditioner"
• -heater	• -heater	• -"air conditioning"

Pitfall 3: Budget Hogs

You may have a set of ad groups that fall under a single campaign with a $100 daily budget. There are no issues with the campaign settings, but one ad group—perhaps a single keyword within that ad group—uses the majority of the daily budget. Because the extremely popular keyword shares the same budget with all ad groups in the campaign, many keywords miss opportunities to display ads because of the budget constraint.

Start by evaluating the performance of the popular keywords, to see if the traffic is valuable to your business. Chapter 12 covers conversion tracking, which shows if an ad click triggered by a particular keyword resulted in a sale (or a sign-up, or a registration, or whatever constitutes success for your campaign). If you find that a popular keyword does not convert, look for ways to refine it. Chapter 6 covers keyword match types and negative keywords; these may help decrease unprofitable traffic.

If the keyword is a keeper, you can increase the campaign's daily budget to provide additional opportunities for impressions and clicks. But what if the increased budget is monopolized by the same keyword? To give other keywords a chance to compete in the auction, create a new campaign with its own, separate daily budget. Then, move the budget-devouring ad group or keyword into the new campaign. By separating it, other keywords have a chance to run and you control the budget.

CHAPTER 4

Navigating Your Account

Interface Overview

The AdWords user interface is organized into three sections: top navigation, left sidebar, and middle pane.

Spend some time getting used to the interface, keeping in mind that AdWords changes frequently. If you login on a regular basis you can keep up with changes as they roll out.

The top navigation, from here on referred to as "tabs" is shown in Figure 4-1.

Figure 4-1. Top navigation

The top navigation includes six sections: Home, Campaigns, Opportunities, Tools and Analysis, Billing, and "My account." Let's take a look at each section.

Home Tab

This tab, shown in Figure 4-2, provides a snapshot view of the account, including important metrics, alerts, and customizable data points called modules.

The first two modules, "Alerts and announcements" and "Performance graph," cannot be moved or removed. The performance graph provides a visual representation of a metric. The graph displays fluctuations over time to help identify performance dips and spikes. Change the graph to review and compare different metrics, including clicks, impressions, CTR, average CPM, cost, average position, and various conversion metrics. For example, you might want to compare cost to average position, or average position to conversions.

Figure 4-2. The Home tab

Below these modules, customize the page to display data you care about. AdWords provides default modules, including "Keywords below first page bid." Customize the visible modules by clicking the "Customize modules" link at the top left side of the page, then select or deselect modules.

Rearrange modules on the page (see Figure 4-3) by clicking and dragging the dotted icon in the left corner. The icons in the right corner allow you to customize the number of visible data rows, select metrics to display, and minimize or remove the module.

Another important item to note: The data displayed in AdWords is specific to a time frame. Figure 4-3 shows the time frame, displayed in the top right corner. Time frame can also be set in the Campaigns tab.

To change the visible time frame, click the down arrow icon to select the desired option. Presets include:

- Today
- Yesterday
- This week (Sunday–Today)
- This week (Monday–Today)
- Last 7 days
- Last week (Sunday–Saturday)
- Last week (Monday–Sunday)
- Last business week (Monday–Friday)

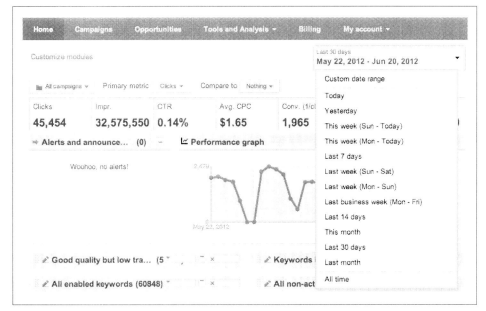

Figure 4-3. Set a time frame

- Last 14 days
- This month
- Last 30 days
- Last month
- All time

Select the option labeled "Custom date range" to create a specific time frame (see Figure 4-4). The drop-down menu changes to two date boxes. Click a box and a calendar appears. Use the arrows to navigate to the desired month, then click the desired date. Once the start date and end date are selected, click the Go button to see the custom view.

When discussing an AdWords account with someone viewing the account on a different computer, you might see different data. The usual culprit is time frame. If you are viewing data for the last seven days and she is looking at data for all time, you will see different numbers.

Campaigns Tab

This tab contains the "meat" of the AdWords account, including campaigns, ad groups, keywords, ad extensions, and placements. The majority of day-to-day account man-

Figure 4-4. Set a custom time frame

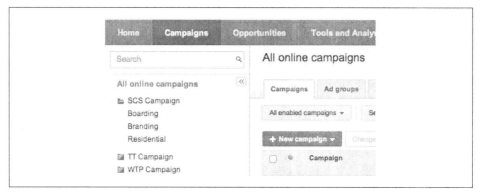

Figure 4-5. Account tree view

agement happens here. There are two ways to navigate within the campaigns tab: the left navigation pane, called the tree view, and a secondary navigation bar above the middle pane, called roll-up tabs.

The Tree View

If an AdWords account has more than one campaign, a vertical navigation area called the tree view appears in the left column. As you see in Figure 4-5, this view displays a link for "All online campaigns." Folder icons appear beneath, each representing a campaign. Click a folder icon to see a list of ad groups associated with that campaign. To view a specific area of the account in the middle pane, click the corresponding name in the tree view.

Minimize or fully display the tree view by clicking the double arrow icon at the top right corner.

The Roll-Up Tabs

Once a campaign or ad group is selected in the tree view you can work within that selection. To do this, use the roll-up tabs above the middle pane shown in Figure 4-6. Each roll-up tab changes the data displayed in the middle pane.

Default roll-up tabs include the following:

Campaigns
   View data at the campaign level; create additional campaigns within the account
Ad groups
   View data at the ad group level; create additional ad groups within a campaign
Settings
   View settings for each campaign (only accessible when a single campaign is selected on the tree view)
Ads
   View data at the ad creative level; add, edit, or delete ad creative
Keywords
   View data at the keyword level; add, edit, or delete keywords; add negative keywords; view the Keyword Details report
Dimensions
   View and segment performance by the dimension of your choice across a campaign, ad group, or the entire account (for example, view statistics by month, hour, or geographic region in a single report)
Display Network (optional, but on by default for campaigns opted in the Display Network)
   View data at the placement level; add or exclude placements and manage placement bids

Optional roll-up tabs include the following:

Ad extensions
   Automatically displays when an ad extension is enabled
Auto targets
   View data for product listing ads served via Google's Merchant Center

Let's look at each roll-up tab in more detail.

Campaigns Roll-Up Tab.   The Campaigns roll-up tab is visible when "All online campaigns" is selected from the tree view. This option displays all campaigns in the account, providing a nice summary of your account. The view can be set to display all campaigns, all enabled campaigns, or all but deleted campaigns.

First, you can see the daily budget per campaign, with a total daily budget at the bottom. Each campaign has a status - there are seven status options. "Eligible" means everything is in good shape, and your ads can show (it's not a guarantee they will show, they still have to compete in the AdWords auction).

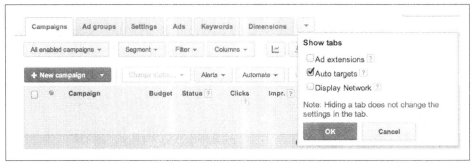

Figure 4-6. Roll-up tabs

A campaign can be "paused," "deleted," or "ended" (interesting to note, you can re-activate a deleted campaign, so this status is essentially the same as paused). "Pending" means the campaign isn't running now, but is scheduled to run at a future date. If you opted to use the prepaid billing option, the campaign status is "suspended" if the pre-paid balance runs out. Last, campaigns can be "Limited by budget." That's essentially the same as eligible, but AdWords is letting you know you could spend much, much more.

Other useful information displayed includes the default maximum cost per click, the number of clicks, impressions, clickthrough rate (CTR), average cost per click, and average position. See more information by clicking the "Columns" link, found beneath the roll-up tab bar. From here, select additional columns to see performance data, conversion data, phone call details, competitive metrics and attributes (labels).

 Each roll-up tab includes the "Columns" link with different options for customizing the view.

Another handy feature: the performance summary graph. This graph is a visual repre-sentation of the campaign performance over a period of time. It can be customized to display various metrics, like clicks, impressions, clickthrough rate, cost, average posi-tion and how they change over time. You can also compare metrics. To customize the graph, click the performance summary graph button ⌐ next to the "Columns" link, shown in Figure 4-7. The graph is available for the Campaigns, Ad groups, Ads, Key-words, Dimensions, and Display Network roll-up tabs.

The Campaigns roll-up tab is also the starting place for creating new campaigns. To begin, click the button labeled "+ New campaign" ⌐+ New campaign ▾⌐, found below the per-formance summary graph. You have many campaign setup options, including Default (ads show everywhere), Search Network only (ads show on Google search and the Search partners), Display Network only, Display Network only (remarketing), Search and Display Networks (mobile devices).

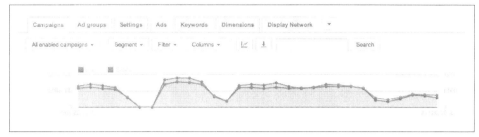

Figure 4-7. Customize the performance summary graph

You can always change campaign settings later. You may notice two additional campaign options: online video and TV campaigns. These campaigns are for running video content on YouTube.com and television. This book's focus is online campaigns.

Let's cover one more roll-up tab tool, the filter. Filters are handy for identifying high and low performers across the account. You can narrow visible data by text search, status, and performance criteria. The feature is available for all roll-up tabs except Settings.

To streamline account management, create saved filters for frequently used views. To create a filter, click the "Filter" link below the roll-up tabs. Here are some ways to use filters:

- From the Campaigns roll-up tab, use a filter to display all campaigns where the average cost per click is greater than or equal to *[insert your number]* See this example in Figure 4-8.
- From the Ad groups roll-up tab, use a filter to display all ad groups where the total conversion value is less than or equal to *[insert your number]*.
- From the Ads roll-up tab, use a filter to display all ads where the average position is worse than *[insert your number]*.
- From the Keywords roll-up tab, use a filter to display all keywords with a Quality Score equal to *[insert your number]*.

Saved filters are module options on the Home tab. To set it up, check the "Save filter" box and give it a recognizable name. On the Home tab, click "Customize modules." The saved filter appears in the list of options.

Use the search box below the roll-up tabs to find words and phrases. This is essentially the same as running a filter for that text.

Ad Groups Roll-Up Tab. The Ad groups roll-up tab is visible if you select "All online campaigns" or an individual campaign from the tree view. This tab displays all ad groups

Figure 4-8. Filter campaigns by average CPC

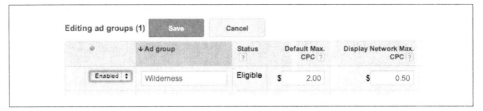

Figure 4-9. Use the Edit button to change values in multiple columns

in the account or the selected campaign. Similar to the Campaigns roll-up tab, it displays a status for each ad group.

Ad groups have additional status options. "Incomplete" status means ads can't run because the ad group is missing critical components like keywords or the ads. Ad groups are subject to the status of the parent campaign. If an enabled ad group cannot show ads because of its campaign, you see a status messages like: "Campaign paused," "Campaign deleted," "Campaign ended," "Campaign suspended," or "Campaign pending."

In addition to the metrics available for campaigns, the Ad groups roll-up tab displays the default maximum CPC, the Display Network maximum CPC and the Max CPP.

New ad groups are created from the Ad groups roll-up tab. To begin, click the button labeled "+ New ad group" ![+ New ad group], found below the performance summary graph.

The next button is labeled "Edit." Start by selecting check boxes next to ad groups you wish to edit. Select all rows by checking the box at the top of the header row. Now, the Edit button becomes active and you can make changes, inline, to all selected ad groups as shown in Figure 4-9. Or, skip this step and click directly on the columns and rows you want to edit as shown in Figure 4-10. With inline changes, edits happen one-by-one.

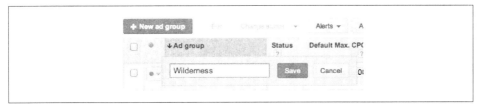

Figure 4-10. Click individual columns to make edits inline

Figure 4-11. To make a bulk status change, select multiple ad groups, then choose the desired status

Similarly, you can change the status for each ad group individually or make bulk changes using the "Change status..." button shown in Figure 4-11. This button becomes active when an ad group's checkbox is selected. Status options include Enabled, Paused and Deleted. Each option is color coded for easy identification.

Another useful feature is "Alerts," found in the navigation bar below the performance summary graph. Alerts are available in Campaigns, Ad groups, Ads, and Keywords roll-up tabs. You can create and manage custom alerts based on events significant to the account. For example, you might want an alert when 75 percent of the daily budget has been spent, as in Figure 4-12, or when the average position drops below four. Alerts display messages in the account interface or send email when specified conditions are met. Alerts can monitor the account daily, weekly or continually (every few hours).

Create a custom alert

Custom alerts can help keep track of changes that are important to you. Triggered alerts will appear in the messages section above.

Alert type	Percent of Daily Budget Spent ▾	> ▾ 75 %
Check	Continually (every few hours) ▾	
Apply to	○ Selected ad groups	
	○ Every ad group in this campaign	
	⦿ Campaign	
Additional notifications	☑ Email	

[Create] [Cancel]

Figure 4-12. Create custom alerts

The AdWords interface rolled out a facelift during the week of June 18, 2012. Most functionality seems the same. However, the custom alerts feature no longer works. If you had existing alerts, they are still there, but as of this printing you cannot create new alerts. AdWords engineers typically address bugs quickly, so this may be resolved soon. The screenshot in Figure 4-12 shows the previous interface.

Settings Roll-Up Tab. Settings are applied at the campaign level. To access this roll-up tab, select "All online campaigns" or an individual campaign folder icon from the tree view. From here, you view and manage campaign settings. Settings govern high level campaigns decisions; Chapter 5 covers this topic in detail. Let's move along to the next roll-up tab.

Ads Roll-Up Tab. The Ads roll-up tab displays all ad creative associated with the campaign or ad group selected in the tree view. Like previous tabs, you can edit ads inline, create new ads, change status, and create custom alerts.

Let's look at another useful feature, labeled "Automate." The Automate button leads to an AdWords feature called automated rules. Automated rules save time by scheduling automatic changes based on specified criteria. So, how can you use them?

Scheduling
Turn campaigns, ads groups or ads on or off on a schedule or for promotional events.

Pause low-performers
Pause low-performing campaigns, ad groups, ads, and keywords.

Bid adjustments
Adjust bids for keywords based on cost per conversion; change bids for a desired average position; raise bids to show ads on the first page; bid scheduling (e.g., a higher bid during certain hours of the day).

Control budgets and cost
Budget scheduling (e.g. higher budget on certain days of the week); pause campaigns that have spent a certain budget partway through the month; increase the budget for campaigns that convert well (using cost-per-conversion data).

AdWords allows up to 100 rules per account. Let's set one up.

Start by finding the Automate button, on the navigation bar below the performance graph   Automate ▾ .

Automate is available for Campaigns, Ad groups, Ads, and Keywords roll-up tabs, each with different sets of applicable rules. In the Ads roll-up tab, you can pause or enable ads based on criteria you set. In this example, let's pause ads when the cost per conversion exceeds $50. The rule runs once per week, considering conversion data from the past 30 days. Give the rule a name to identify it, and set it to email a notification every time it runs. It looks like Figure 4-13.

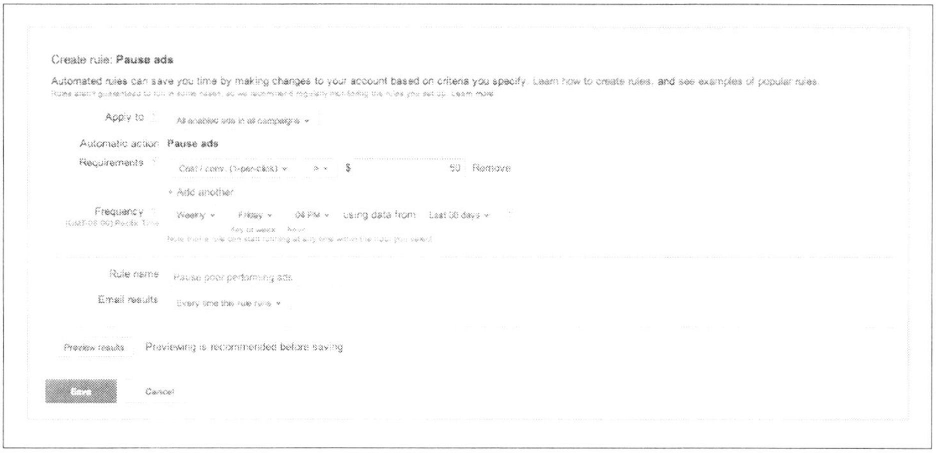

Figure 4-13. Set up an automated rule for ads

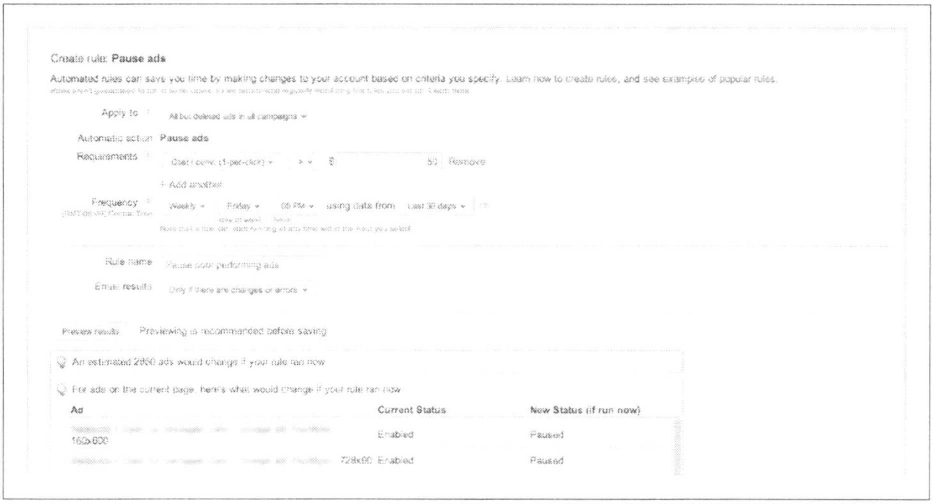

Figure 4-14. Before saving an automated rule, preview the results

Automated rules have the potential to make significant changes to the account. It's important to be thoughtful and thorough when setting them up. Be sure to preview the rule before you save it. Figure 4-14 shows what the rule would change if it ran now.

To view rules in the account, look under the tree view for a separate section labeled "Automated rules." From here you can edit, pause and delete existing rules (but you can't create new rules). You see a log of activity showing which rules ran, when they ran, and what changed, If a rule runs afoul, this is the area to fix it. To revert, click the "Undo..." button in the Logs table. You can undo the most recent changes made by each rule, and backtrack, undoing each set of changes one by one. There is no "redo." Take a look at this section in Figure 4-15.

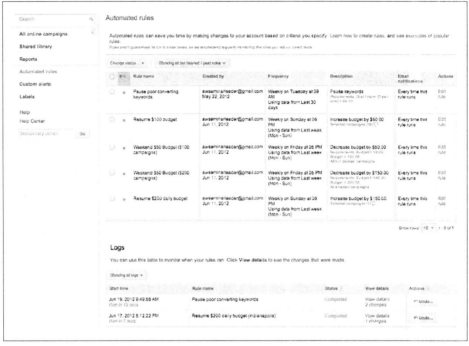

Figure 4-15. Automated rules appear in the tree view

 To learn more about automated rules, including popular examples, visit the AdWords Help Center *http://goo.gl/q1DND*

Keywords Roll-Up Tab. The Keywords roll-up tab includes two sections: keywords that trigger ads, and keywords that prevent ads from appearing, called negative keywords. The interface separates these two types to simplify management.

Like the previous roll-up tabs, the Keywords tab includes a performance summary graph and features like add, edit, alerts, and automate. This topic merits a separate chapter; Chapter 6.

Before moving on, let's cover one additional feature: Labels. You can create labels from the roll-up tabs, or in the Labels section under the tree view.

Labels enable the creation of custom groupings in the account. Consider an account with several campaigns and different geotargets. Each campaign has the same set of keywords, but statistics are only viewable campaign-by-campaign. To see how identical keywords perform across multiple campaigns, create a label to group them into a set.

Figure 4-16. Create and manage labels from the Labels section

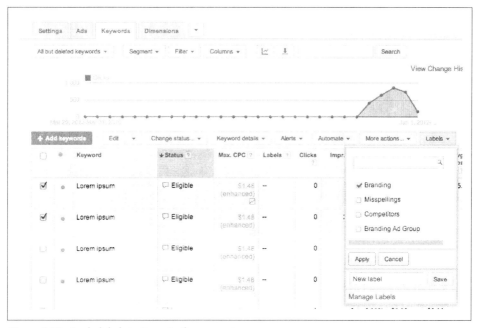

Figure 4-17. Apply labels to items in the account

Let's say you want to compare the performance of branded keywords and competitor keywords. Start by creating labels for each category, as shown in Figure 4-16.

Now, select the keywords from the account and apply the appropriate label as shown in Figure 4-17.

Once labels are created and sections of the account tagged you can generate reports. Let's move on to the next roll-up tab, Dimensions, to learn more.

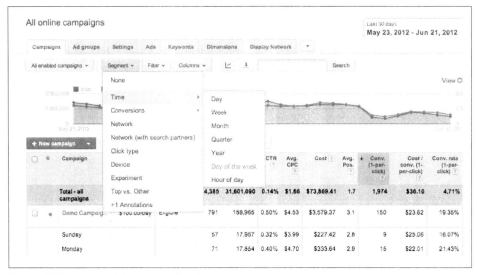

↑Label	Clicks ?	Impr. ?	CTR ?	Avg. CPC ?	Cost ?	Avg. Pos. ?	Conv. (1-per-click) ?	Cost / conv. (1-per-click) ?	Conv. rate (1-per-click) ?
■ Branding	40	1,837	2.18%	$2.26	$90.23	4.2	6	$14.51	15.38%
Competitors	0	76	0.00%	$0.00	$0.00	3.3	0	$0.00	0.00%
Everything else ?	45,413	32,573,637	0.14%	$1.65	$75,009.62	1.7	1,960	$36.89	4.57%

Figure 4-18. The Dimensions roll-up tab displays data across tabs

Figure 4-19. Segment data by day of week

Dimensions Roll-Up Tab. The Dimensions roll-up tab lets you create custom views across an ad group, campaign, or the account. This feature makes it easy to compare performance across campaigns. There are many dimensions available, including time, day, geographic location, search terms and more. Labels can be viewed as dimensions, as shown in Figure 4-18. This report shows that branded keywords out-perform competitor keywords.

If you do not need to compare data across campaigns, another option for viewing a performance breakdown is the "Segment" link shown in Figure 4-19.

Segments are available for campaigns, ad groups, ads, or keywords; the options vary depending on what roll-up tab is viewed. Example segments include:

- Campaign data by network, click type, device, and experiments
- Ad group data by day, week, month, quarter, year or day of week

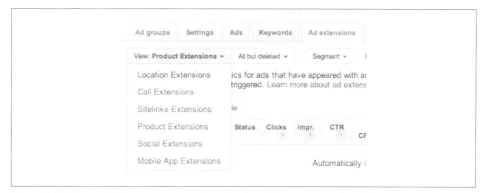

Figure 4-20. Access different extensions from the drop-down menu under Ad extensions

- Keyword data by search term match type

Use this data to optimize campaigns. For example, if performance differs significantly on a network, device, keyword, or day of week, make adjustments to capitalize on profitable traffic and filter irrelevant traffic.

Display Network Roll-Up Tab

The Display Network roll-up tab manages ads on the Google Display Network. It shows which websites, web pages, mobile apps, and more—called placements—your ads appeared on. In 2012, the interface changed to group Display Keywords, Placements, Topics, and Interests & Remarketing tabs under this tab.

Chapter 9 covers Google Display Network features.

Ad Extensions Roll-Up Tab

The "Ad Extensions" roll-up tab provides access to different extensions—or add-ons —for your ads. Extensions include location extensions for displaying address information with ads; call extensions for displaying trackable phone numbers with ads; sitelinks extensions for displaying additional links below text ads; product extensions for connecting AdWords with a corresponding Google Merchant Center account; social extensions to connecting with a Google+ page, and mobile app extensions, which can target visitors in an App Store (like Google Play and the Apple App Store).

To access this roll-up tab, look for the gray shaded box beneath the roll-up tabs, in the left corner. Click the arrow and select the extension you wish to view. The middle pane changes to reflect the extension you wish to work on. Check out Figure 4-20 to see how it looks in an AdWords account.

Chapter 8 covers ad extensions in more detail.

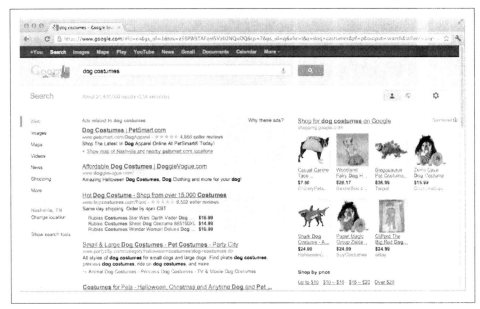

Figure 4-21. Product listing ads at the top right corner of a Google search results page

Autotargets Roll-Up Tab

The Autotargets roll-up tab is applicable to eCommerce websites that list products in Google's Merchant Center (*http://goo.gl/WC5Gj*). This tab provides a way to display product images on Google's search results pages. There are two types of associated ads: product listing ads and product extensions.

Product listing ads show a product image, title, price, and the business name, as shown in Figure 4-21. This format is available in the United States, U.K., Germany, and France. This standalone ad format targets is designed to connect shoppers directly with appropriate products. All information displayed in ads is pulled from the Merchant Center account.

To show product listing ads, you must link your AdWords account to a Google Merchant Center account. You can target specific sets of products from the Merchant Center with AdWords campaigns. AdWords compares search queries with the product attributes assigned in the Merchant Center. Ads are ranked on bid, relevancy to the search query, and historical performance. Like standard ads, you are charged on a cost-per-click basis, based on bids defined at the ad group level or for particular product targets.

Product listing ads are managed through an optional roll-up tab labeled "Auto targets" (Figure 4-22). Auto targets allow you to specify which Merchant Center products are eligible for display and to set specific bids for each target. Auto targets support filters, to exclude particular products from your feed.

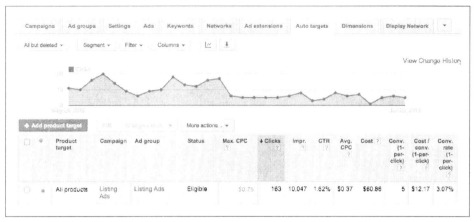

Figure 4-22. Auto targets for product listing ads

 To learn more about setting up product listing ads, visit the AdWords
Help center at *http://goo.gl/nvxfL*. You will see detailed documentation
for setting it up, including instructions for creating a product feed and
the required product attributes to be eligible for product listing ads.

The second option for showing images on Google search results pages is called product
extensions. This is not a standalone format; images are shown with a standard text ad.
Unlike product listing ads, which are shopper-focused, product extensions are mer-
chant-focused, designed to give searchers a sense of the advertiser's products.

If you connect your AdWords account to a Merchant Center Account, both types of
ads are eligible to run. To use product listing ads without enabling extensions, remove
all keywords or text ads from the campaign. Why? Because product extensions appear
with regular text ads that trigger on keywords. Ads and keywords are irrelevant for
product listing ads, which use information from your data feed in the Merchant Center
account.

Chapter 8 covers product extensions in detail.

Opportunities

The Opportunities tab provides three optimization tools: Ideas, Campaign bid simulator, and Analyze competition. The default view is Ideas, and the others are accessed
from the tree view. Let's take a look at each.

Ideas

Ideas are automatically generated by the AdWords software every two weeks. If you check back periodically there are new suggestions based on activity from the last time period.

First, specify the optimization goal from the drop-down menu. There are three options: Increase traffic, Balance cost and traffic, and Maintain or decrease cost. If you select Increase traffic, the suggestions should increase the number of clicks, but costs may increase significantly. The second option offers a middle ground, with suggestions that can increase the number of clicks without large budget changes. The third option offers suggestions for improvements within the existing budget.

Next, select the type of suggestions to view: bids, budgets, sitelinks, or keywords, displayed as green tabs like this .

The Bids and Budgets tabs presents a list of campaigns and ad groups that could benefit from changes to the daily budget or max CPC bid. It suggests a new (higher) amount and indicates how many additional clicks the ad group can expect from the change. Clicking a specific suggestion displays a detailed breakout of the potential impact of the idea, shown in Figure 4-23. The chart and graph show estimates of how different bids and budgets would impact the number of daily clicks, cost, and cost per click. You can change the campaign budget from this screen.

The Sitelinks tab shows a list of campaigns that are eligible to show sitelinks, but don't have them. It shows a preview of what the ad would look like if sitelinks were added and an estimate of the additional cost and clicks.

The Keywords tab provides lists of potential new keywords by ad group. You see estimates for cost, impressions, and clicks the account could expect if the keywords are added. Similar to the Budget ideas option, click a suggestion to get more detail, including a list of the suggested keywords, potential cost, clicks, and competition. You can select some, all, or none of the suggestions.

> Remember, these suggestions are created by an automated system, and may not be appropriate for your business. Do not add ideas without carefully reviewing first.

If you are unsure about a proposed idea, try an experiment. Take a look at Figure 4-24. You see a checkbox labeled "Not ready? Run experiment." below the keyword suggestions. Checking this box automatically applies the selected keywords to 50 percent of the ad traffic. The experiment can run for as little as seven days; the maximum duration is 90 days.

You see experiment results in the Ideas section. If the results are good, apply the ideas to the account at any time. If results are poor, delete the experiment. Be sure to monitor

Figure 4-23. Budget ideas show how different daily budgets impact campaign traffic

progress; if you do not delete it the experimental keywords go live at the conclusion of the experiment.

Campaign Bid Simulator

The bid simulator provides estimates showing how bid changes can impact traffic. It's neat because it essentially recreates the auction from the past week, showing what might have happened if bids were different. The tool uses data from the past seven days on the Search Network only, not the Display Network. Figure 4-25 shows how traffic would change based on a max CPC changes ranging from -50 percent to +300 percent.

You have two ways to view the data: bid scaling or campaign-wide bid. Bid scaling simulates what could have happened if all bids had been changed by a specified percentage. Campaign-wide bid simulates what could have happened if all keyword bids were removed and all ad group bids were set to a single value. You can download the data as a *.csv* file by clicking the "Download simulation data" button. To implement a bid change, select the desired radio button and click "Apply now."

One frustration: often you will not see suggestions. The most common culprit is budget. If a campaign hits (or comes close to) the daily budget at any point in the last week, you won't see estimates. Other reasons suggestions won't appear: the simulator doesn't work with campaigns using automatic CPC bidding or Conversion Optimizer; cam-

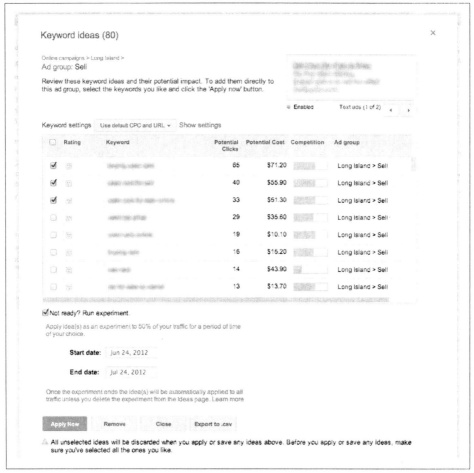

Figure 4-24. An experiment applies half your traffic to the keyword ideas

paigns with advanced ad scheduling; campaigns without enough data, and ad groups that use keyword-level bids.

Analyze Competition

The Analyze Competition tool shows how your account performs compared to other advertisers. The report is broken down by specific categories and subcategories, comparing performance based on impressions, clicks, clickthrough rate, and average position. You can't see raw data, but the report provides a competitive range bar, broken into five segments. The reports shows—by metric—whether the account ranks in the top, middle, or bottom of the competitive range. Figure 4-26 shows this advertiser is at the top of the competitive range for impressions in the Vehicles category.

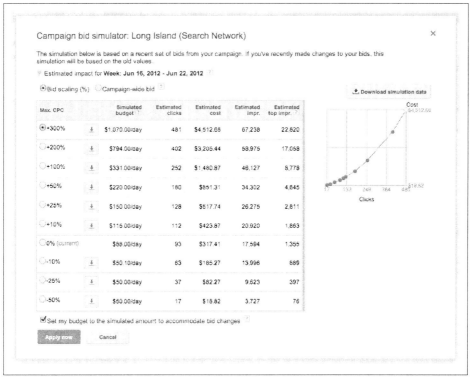

Figure 4-25. The bid simulator shows how bid changes could impact traffic and cost

Figure 4-26. Analyze competition shows where you rank compared to other advertisers bidding on the same types of keywords

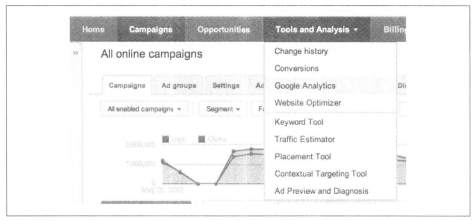

Figure 4-27. Access a variety of tools from the "Tools and Analysis" tab

Clicking the main categories displays subcategory breakdowns. At the end of the line, you reach a list of the most common search queries from the category that triggered ads. Based on the statistics, you can add the queries as positive or negative keywords.

Tools and Analysis

The "Tools and Analysis" tab shown in Figure 4-27 does not have a standalone section, but provides access to important AdWords tools. These include:

- Change history
- Conversion Tracking, covered in Chapter 12
- Google Analytics, introduced in Chapter 12
- Website Optimizer (available until August 1, 2012; relocating to Google Analytics after that date)
- Keyword Tool, covered in Chapter 6
- Traffic Estimator, covered in Chapter 11
- Placement Tool, covered in Chapter 9
- Contextual Targeting Tool, covered in Chapter 9
- Preview and Diagnosis

Let's take a look at some of the tools available in this section.

Change History

Change history, shown in Figure 4-28, shows a comprehensive list of account changes, broken down by date. Adjust the view to see all changes, or changes to budgets, cost per click, keywords, status, distribution (networks), targeting (geotargets), and ads.

Figure 4-28. Change history shows what's changed, who changed it, and when

You see who made the change, with a time and date, by campaign and ad group. The Changes column provides details, including what keywords were added and deleted from the account. This tool includes a performance summary graph to compare performance shifts to changes made on particular dates. This tool is one of the first places to start for account diagnostics.

 If multiple people work on the same AdWords account, it's a good idea to create unique logins for each person. That way, you can track who made changes. If you hire an agency to manage your AdWords account, use this tool to monitor changes they make on your behalf.

Ad Preview and Diagnosis

The Ad Preview and Diagnosis tool, shown in Figure 4-29, shows a preview of a Google search results page. You can specify the Google domain, language, location, and targeted device. Then, it tells you whether your ads are triggering on the test search query.

Below, you see a Google search results page, with a "Preview" step and repeat watermark in the background. If your ad appears, it's highlighted in green.

One big advantage of the tool is that it does not accrue statistics, so you won't inflate impressions and hurt CTR. One downside: clicking the ads does not take you to the landing page. So, you can read competitors' ads, but you can't visit their websites from this tool.

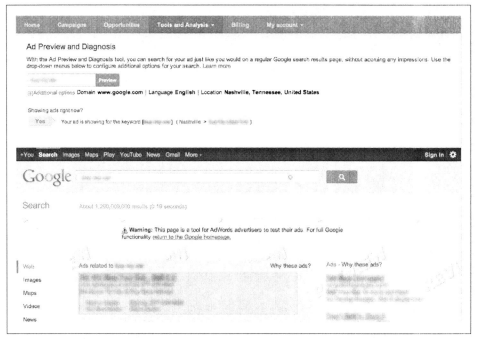

Figure 4-29. The Ad Preview and Diagnosis tool shows whether your ad appears on Google, without accruing statistics

 This tool is available externally at *http://goo.gl/K21xf*. Unlike the version in AdWords, the external tool does not show data specific to an AdWords account.

Billing

This Billing tab includes three sections: Transaction History, Billing settings, and Billing profile. Let's take a look at each.

Transaction History

The Transaction history, shown in Figure 4-30 shows a list of every charge, including the date, the number of clicks, debits, credits, and balance. From this section, you can do the following:

- Make a payment
- Add a promotional code (click the "More actions" button)
- View transactions by cost, earnings, payments, adjustments, and taxes
- View detailed report or a summary of activity

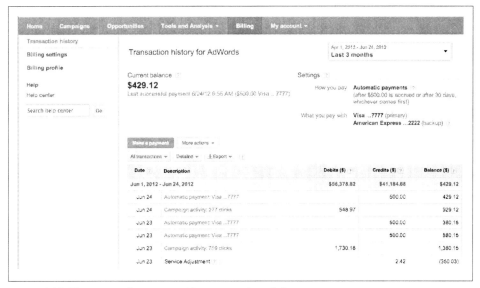

Figure 4-30. Transaction history provides an overview of charges

- Export data as a *.csv* file
- See charges campaign-by-campaign by clicking rows labeled "Campaign activity"
- See a printable receipt by clicking rows labeled "Payment"
- See refunds/adjustments applied to the account

Billing Settings

Billing settings, shown in Figure 4-31, display the following:

- Account details (the payee and the nickname for the account)
- Your selections, which includes the payment method and form of payment

From here you can change your billing method and add or edit credit cards or bank accounts. Chapter 11 covers billing in more detail.

Billing Profile

In the billing profile, shown in Figure 4-32, you can edit the billing name, address, and phone number.

My account

The "My account" tab includes three sections: Account access, Notification settings, and Preferences. Let's take a look at each.

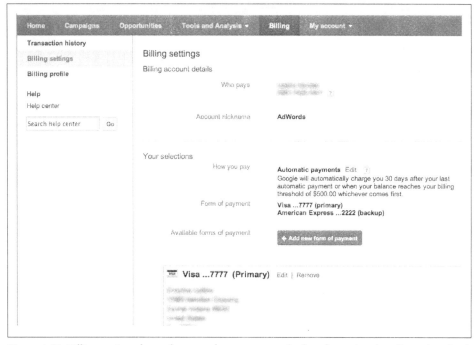

Figure 4-31. Billing settings show who pays, the payment method, and associated credit cards or bank accounts

Account Access

This area, shown in Figure 4-33, provides a summary of who can access the AdWords account. From here you can:

- See a list of users with access to the account, when the last logged in, and the access level.
- See if the account has an associated client manager, when the account was linked, and the access type.
- Invite others to access the account.

Notification Settings

The Notification settings section, shown in Figure 4-34, shows the email address where account notifications are sent and notification preferences. Notifications are categorized like this:

- Billing alerts
- Disapproved ads and policy alerts
- Campaign maintenance alerts

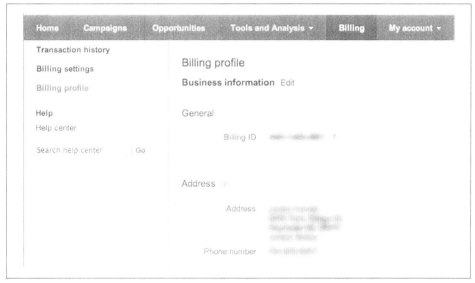

Figure 4-32. Edit the billing name, address, and phone number in the billing profile

Figure 4-33. Account access shows who can login to the account

- Reports
- Customized help and performance suggestions
- Newsletters
- Google market research
- Special offers

You cannot opt out of the first three notifications, but you can reduce email from AdWords by changing the status from "All" to "Only critical." The other categories can be changed by clicking the notification setting. For example, to stop Special offers

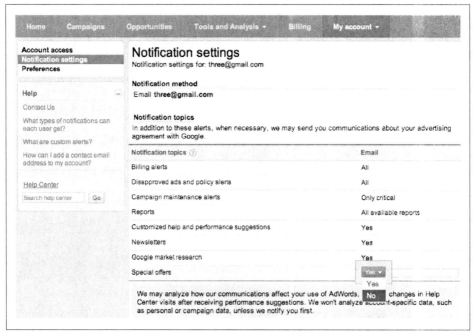

Figure 4-34. Notification settings let you control how much AdWords can email you

emails, click the "Yes" status which reveals a drop-down menu. Now, change the value to "No" and the account is opted out of that notification.

Preferences

The final section, labeled Preferences, looks like Figure 4-35. Preferences is an eclectic group. First, it shows the time zone associated with the account. This cannot be changed once the account is created. If you use ad scheduling, it's important to note the account's time zone.

The second section, labeled Tracking, lets you turn auto-tagging on and off. Auto-tagging automatically tags ad destination URLs with tracking information required to see AdWords data in Google Analytics reports. If you don't see AdWords data in the reports this is the first place to troubleshoot.

The third section provides a link to Google's Advertising Program Terms.

That's the Tour!

Now that you've made it through this chapter, login to your AdWords account and explore for a while. Once you're comfortable with the user interface, campaign man-

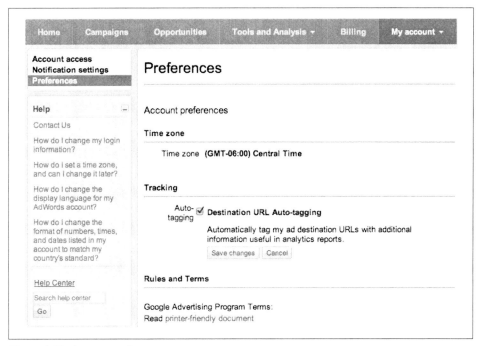

Figure 4-35. Account preferences

agement becomes much easier. Keep in mind that the interface changes frequently, so do not be concerned if the screenshots in this book don't perfectly match what you're seeing. I manage 50+ accounts, and I usually see interface differences across many accounts. Things move and colors change, but the functionality usually remains the same.

The next chapters cover information you need to be successful within this system.

CHAPTER 5

Campaign Settings

Introduction to Campaign Settings

Campaign settings control administrative decisions for your AdWords account. Selected at the campaign level, they apply to all ad groups within the campaign.

Many advertisers struggle when deciding whether to create a new campaign or an ad group within an existing campaign. The answer is simple: if all the settings for the existing campaign are applicable, create a new ad group within the campaign. If different settings are required, including a separate budget, create a new campaign. This chapter explains how each Settings affects the ad groups within.

Each campaign requires a unique name. This name does not impact performance in the AdWords auction in any way, but a logical naming convention can make your life easier. The default name for a new campaign is "Campaign #[numeral]." A better practice is to label each campaign by its defining attributes. For example, if the new campaign is destined to show ads to searchers in Nashville, Tenn. on the Google Display Network, an appropriate name might be "Nashville—GDN." Another campaign targeting Knoxville, Tenn. and Google Search might be labeled "Knoxville—Search Only." The campaign name is up to you, but clear labels make account management easier.

Let's review campaign settings that impact the AdWords auction.

Locations and Languages

Campaigns control where in the world ads are eligible to display and what browser languages they target. Let's look at this section in more detail.

Figure 5-1. Location targeting

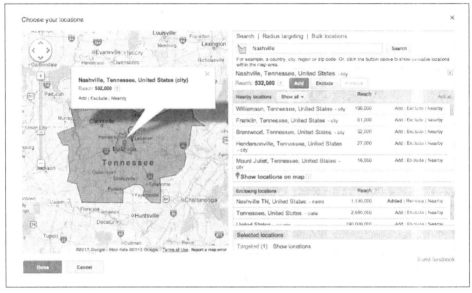

Figure 5-2. Choose locations where ads can display

Location Targeting

The Locations and Languages section shown in Figure 5-1 allows you to specify where in the world ads are eligible to appear. The defaults vary; most U.S.-based accounts default to the United States or the United States and Canada.

If none of the radio button options are appropriate for the campaign, click the radio button labeled "Let me choose…" Next, type in the name of the desired location in the text box below or click "Advanced search." Now you see locations on a map. Also, you can specify a radius, helpful for brick and mortars and service providers. Figure 5-2 shows location suggestions for Nashville, Tenn.

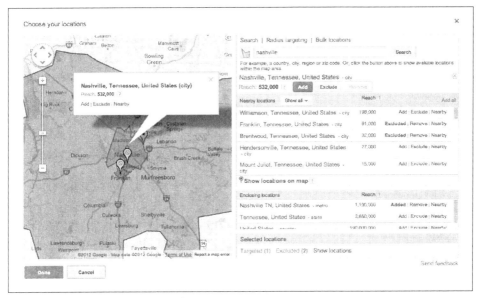

Figure 5-3. Exclusion within targeted area

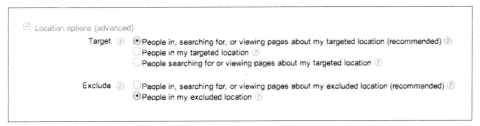

Figure 5-4. Advanced location options

You can exclude areas within the selection by clicking the "Exclude" link next to each location suggestion. In Figure 5-3, ads show to people in metro Nashville, but Franklin and Brentwood, Tenn. are excluded.

Advanced Location Options

AdWords allows advanced targeting and exclusion options. These options are labeled "Location options (advanced)" shown in Figure 5-4. If you use the default inclusion option, "Target using either physical location or search intent (recommended)," ads display to searchers physically located in the targeted area, as well as searchers who include location-specific search terms in their queries. Other options include targeting by physical location or search intent.

There are two categories: target and exclude.

In the target section, there are three radio button options. The default, labeled "People in, searching for or viewing pages about my targeted location (recommended)" means your ads are shown to:

- People physically located in the targeted location
- People who search for results in your target area, no matter where they are. Example: a searcher in Houston looking for a hotel in Nashville, Tenn.
- People who view web pages on the Google Display Network about the targeted location, no matter where they are. Example: a person in Houston reading a website about tours in Nashville, Tenn.

If the second option, "People in my targeted area" is selected, ads are displayed to people physically located in the targeted location, even if the search query or topics indicate interest in other locations.

The third option, "People searching for or viewing pages about my targeted location," restricts ads to people who specify by their search queries that they want to find something in the target area. The actual physical location of the searcher is irrelevant; Google will only restrict ads to people in the same country.

So how can you use these options? Let's assume your campaign targets the state of Tennessee. The default option means that searchers within the state, as well as searchers who include Tennessee-specific terms in their queries (regardless of their physical location) are eligible to see the ads.

For example, a searcher in Nashville, Tenn. can see ads. A searcher in Burlington, Vt., can see ads if the search query includes Tennessee-specific terms (e.g., biking routes in tennessee).

If "People in my targeted area" is selected, only searchers physically located in Tennessee can see ads. A searcher in Vermont cannot see the ad, even if the search query includes Tennessee or exactly matches a keyword. See an illustration in Table 5-1.

Table 5-1. People in my targeted location

Target Location	Keyword	Search Query	Searcher Location	Sees Ad?
Tennessee	TN bike routes	bike route tennessee	Nashville, Tenn.	Yes
Tennessee	TN bike routes	bike route tennessee	Atlanta	No

People searching for or viewing pages about my targeted location means the search query or content on the website must explicitly specify location, no matter where the person is located. A searcher in Tennessee looking for bike route information cannot see the ad unless she includes "Tennessee" or a variant as part of the query. See an illustration in Table 5-2.

Table 5-2. People searching for or viewing pages about my targeted location

Target Location	Keyword	Search Query	Searcher Location	Sees Ad?
Tennessee	bike routes	bike route tennessee	Nashville, Tenn.	Yes
Tennessee	bike routes	bike route	Nashville, Tenn.	No
Tennessee	bike routes	bike route TN	Atlanta	Yes
Tennessee	bike routes	bike route TN	Winnipeg, Canada	No—AdWords restricts by country

The second category is labeled exclude.

There are two options: "People in, searching for, or viewing pages about my excluded location (recommended)" and "People in my excluded location." The default means ads won't appear for people physically located in excluded locations. In addition, ads cannot appear for people who search for or view pages about the excluded locations.

The second radio button means ads cannot show for people physically located in excluded locations. But, ads could appear for people outside excluded locations who show interest in the excluded locations.

Let's look at an example.

An advertiser in Nashville, Tenn. has a successful local marketing program but wants to use AdWords for promotion in areas beyond. This exclusion option prevents ads from appearing in the local area. A searcher in Memphis, Tenn. who includes `Nashville` in a query can see ads; a searcher in the excluded location (Nashville) cannot. See an illustration in Table 5-3.

Table 5-3. Exclusion by people in my excluded location

Target Location	Excluded Location	Keyword	Search Query	Searcher Location	Sees Ad?
Tennessee	Nashville	bike route	bike route	Memphis, Tenn.	Yes
Tennessee	Nashville	bike route	bike route Nashville	Memphis, Tenn.	Yes
Tennessee	Nashville	bike route	bike route	Nashville, Tenn.	No

 Visit the AdWords Help Center at *http://goo.gl/sxCa7* for more details and examples about advanced location targeting.

Languages

The AdWords interface allows you to select multiple languages for each campaign (see Figure 5-5), but it displays ads to searchers as-written. You can select English and Spanish as language targets, but ads display in the language you write them in. For this reason, it's a good idea to create separate campaigns for each language.

Figure 5-5. Language options

The language displayed on Google's search results pages is a browser preference controlled by the individual searcher. For example, a searcher in Nashville, Tenn. might search Google.com but sets the interface language to Spanish, as in Figure 5-6. In this case, ads targeting Spanish should appear. If the campaign settings specify Spanish and the ad is written in another language, AdWords may display it, but it does not translate it.

Figure 5-6. Google.com with Spanish interface

A searcher on Google.com.mx with English browser settings should see ads targeted to English. As you see in Figure 5-7, ads can display in different languages on the search results page.

Figure 5-7. Google.com.mx with English interface

Networks and Devices

The Networks and Devices section is perhaps the least newbie-friendly campaign setting. When creating a new campaign, the networks section is preselected to "All available sites" followed by this note in the interface: "(Recommended for new advertisers)." See Figure 5-8.

Figure 5-8. "Networks" defaults to all available sites

If you're new to AdWords, you should do the *opposite* and turn this network off. Here's why. The Display Network is an entirely different beast than Google Search. Your keyword lists are different. Ads and bids may be different. And expectations and goals should be different.

Consider this: A person has a colony of unwanted bats in his attic, so he searches Google for `bat relocation Nashville`. A business specializing in humane wildlife removal bids on that keyword and displays a relevant ad at the moment the searcher needs the service. Perfect! That business has a great chance of acquiring a new customer.

Now, consider the GDN. In this case, the person did not search for bat removal. In fact, she might *love* bats, and visit www.HGTV.com (*http://goo.gl/4zPmC*) for tips on attracting them (see Figure 5-9). In this case, the GDN can display ads contextually relevant to bats, but irrelevant for that visitor.

The point is, the person who sees the ad might not want what you have. Or, she might not be in the buying cycle at that moment. AdWords has millions of placements to display ads, so there is a very real potential to burn through a budget via the Display

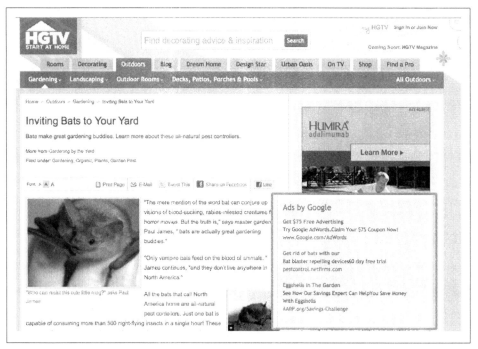

Figure 5-9. Ads on the Google Display Network

Network. Many placements work well for long-term branding strategy campaigns; others do not generate profitable traffic and should be excluded. Monitoring and managing placements is a lot of work, requiring attention and different optimization strategies.

If you're brand new to online advertising, start with the campaign settings shown in Figure 5-10. Get comfortable using AdWords. Then create a separate, experimental campaign targeting the Google Display Network. Chapter 9 covers this network in more detail.

Devices controls where ads can display, including desktop and laptop computers, mobile devices with full browsers, and tablets with full browsers. Like networks, all devices are enabled by default, as shown in Figure 5-11. If you want to target mobile devices, it merits a separate campaign.

Why? Consider how searching on a phone differs from searching on the full-size keyboard. Searches on mobile devices are usually shorter and more location-specific. A searcher on a phone is often looking for something nearby, a place to eat or shop. In this regard, the keywords, ads, and landing page (after all, it has to look good on a phone) may be different than non-mobile campaigns.

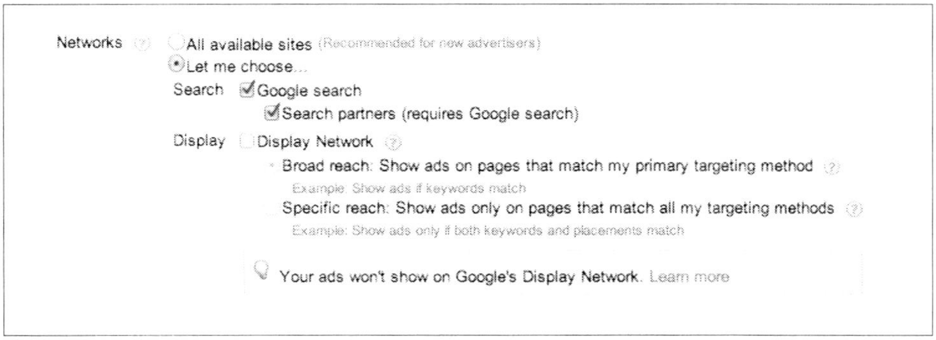

Figure 5-10. If you're new to AdWords, start by targeting Search only

Devices ? ⦿ All available devices (Recommended for new advertisers)
              ○ Let me choose...

Figure 5-11. Click "Let me choose..." to separate computers and mobile devices

Clicking "Let me choose..." reveals all the device options, plus advanced options, including operating systems, device models and carriers and Wi-Fi, shown in Figure 5-12. Wi-Fi traffic shows ads on mobile devices connected to Wi-Fi networks, not specific carriers.

Devices ?   ○ All available devices (Recommended for new advertisers)
            ● Let me choose...
                ☑ Desktop and laptop computers
                ☑ Mobile devices with full browsers
                ☑ Tablets with full browsers

                ⊟ Advanced mobile and tablet options

                    Operating systems ?
                        ○ All available operating systems
                        ● Let me choose...   **Selected operating systems**

                            Android
                            Select versions   Add all
                            BlackBerry
                            Select versions   Add all
                            iOS
                            Select versions   Add all
                            webOS
                            Select versions   Add all

                    Device models ?
                        ○ All available devices
                        ● Let me choose...   **Selected device models**

                            ⊞ Android
                            ⊞ iOS

                    Carriers and Wi-Fi ?
                        ○ All available carriers and Wi-Fi
                        ● Let me choose...   **Selected carriers**

                            ⊼ Wifi   Add
                            ⊞ Canada   Add all
                            ⊞ United States   Add all

Figure 5-12. Advanced mobile and tablet options

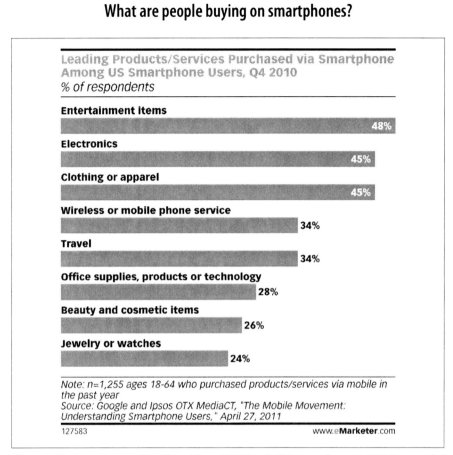

What are people buying on smartphones?

Leading Products/Services Purchased via Smartphone Among US Smartphone Users, Q4 2010
% of respondents

Entertainment items
48%

Electronics
45%

Clothing or apparel
45%

Wireless or mobile phone service
34%

Travel
34%

Office supplies, products or technology
28%

Beauty and cosmetic items
26%

Jewelry or watches
24%

Note: n=1,255 ages 18-64 who purchased products/services via mobile in the past year
Source: Google and Ipsos OTX MediaCT, "The Mobile Movement: Understanding Smartphone Users," April 27, 2011
127583   www.eMarketer.com

Figure 5-13. *According to a Google and Ipsos OYX MediaCT report from April 2011, provided by eMarketer, entertainment items are the leading products purchased via U.S. smartphones in the fourth quarter of 2010.*

Bidding and Budget

The Bidding and budget section allows you to specify the bidding model, default bid, and daily budget for the campaign. Bidding options are covered in Chapter 11. If you're a newbie, select "I'll manually set my bids for clicks." The same option is available in Advanced options, found under the "Focus on clicks—use maximum CPC bids" section, shown in Figure 5-14.

The default bid is the maximum cost per click bid for the ad group. If this is a new campaign, the ad group is created in the next step.

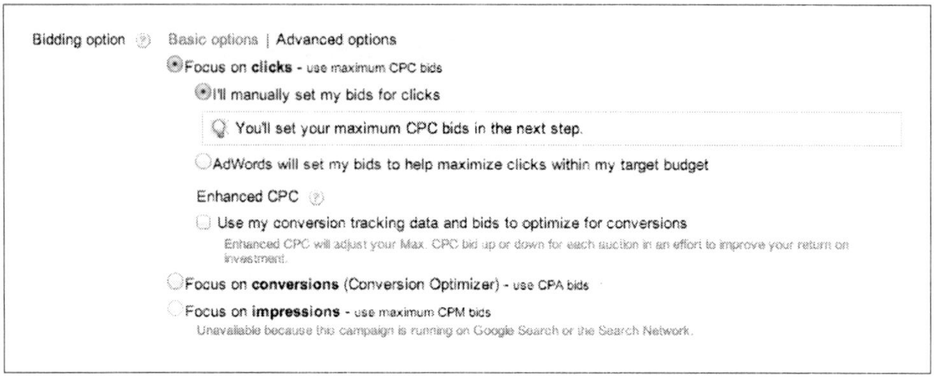

Figure 5-14. Bidding options

The budget is a whole dollar amount with a $1 daily minimum. Keep in mind that this budget applies to this campaign only. If the account has multiple campaigns, the total daily ad spending is the sum of spent budget across all campaigns. The higher the campaign budget, the more opportunities keywords have to display ads throughout the day. AdWords won't penalize you for a small budget; a limited budget simply means that keywords compete in fewer auctions throughout the day.

Delivery Method

Beneath the budget section is a subsection labeled "Delivery method (advanced)." Figure 5-15 shows the options: Standard (the default) and Accelerated.

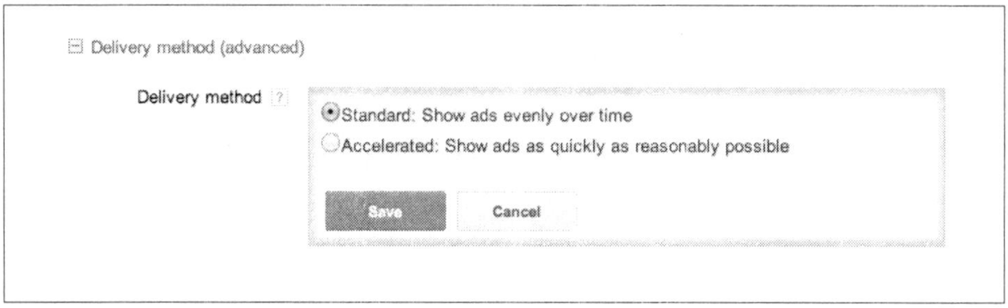

Figure 5-15. Delivery method

Standard delivery means that AdWords tries to display ads as evenly as possible over a 24-hour period, working within the allocated budget. This 24-hour period is based on a midnight-to-midnight schedule, using the time zone selected when the account was created.

Let's assume the campaign contains keywords that can result in millions of ad impressions each day. Based on the average CTR for the keywords, AdWords estimates the number of probable clicks. If the campaign budget is sufficient to cover all estimated

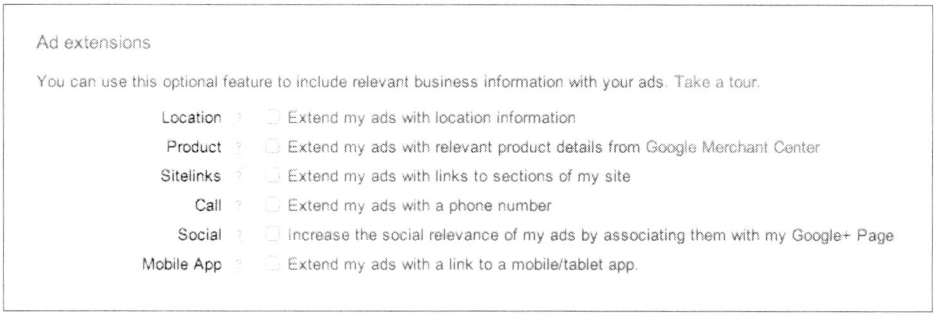

Figure 5-16. Ad extensions can be enabled for new campaigns

clicks, AdWords tries to display ads for every relevant search query. But what if the campaign budget isn't sufficient to cover the estimated clicks? What if the advertiser can afford only 25 clicks per day? In this case, AdWords staggers the ad delivery over 24 hours to ration the budget. This is a common reason why you may not see your ads when searching Google—it's possible that the particular auction did not include you.

The other option is accelerated delivery. This shows ads as quickly as possible, no matter how small the budget. In this case, AdWords shows ads until the daily campaign budget is depleted. Then, ads stop serving until the following day.

Ad Extensions

New campaigns have the option to enable ad extensions from the settings area, as shown in Figure 5-16.

For existing campaigns, extensions have to be managed from the "Ad extensions" roll-up tab. Chapter 8 covers this topic in more detail.

Advanced Settings

The final section includes advanced features for fine-tuning the campaign. Let's walk through them.

Schedule: Start Date, End Date, Ad Scheduling

The first section, labeled "Schedule: Start date, end date, ad scheduling" allows you to select an end date for your campaign. By default, the end date is set to none.

The next option, ad scheduling, defaults to "Show ads all days and hours." Use this to turn ads on and off on specific days and hours of the day. For example, if you'd like to run ads only when someone is available to take a phone call, use this feature to turn off ad delivery when the office is closed. On any individual day, you can select up to six time blocks to display ads. This does not change the auction rules; it simply limits when ads are eligible to participate in the auction. The time of day is based on the time zone selected when the account was created, not on the searcher's time zone.

There are two modes for ad scheduling, basic and bid adjustment. Use basic mode to select hours and days. Bid adjustment mode, shown in Figure 5-17, offers the same features, plus the ability to adjust the percentage of the bid. For example, to bid more aggressively from noon until midnight, increase the bid during those time blocks. This improves the chances of winning the AdWords auction, with a higher ad position. If you'd like to show ads on Saturday, but ad position is less important, decrease the bid. You can turn ads off entirely on any given day.

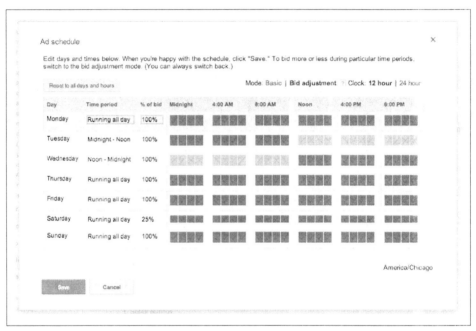

Figure 5-17. Ad scheduling with bid adjustment mode

Ad Delivery: Ad Rotation, Frequency Capping

The next section is labeled "Ad delivery: Ad rotation, frequency capping." Ad rotation offers three options shown in Figure 5-18:

Optimize for clicks (Default)
    Show ads expected to provide more clicks

Optimize for conversions
    Show ads expected to provide more conversions

Rotate
    Show ads more evenly for 90 days, then optimize for clicks

Figure 5-18. Ad rotation options

Ad rotation works by comparing performance of multiple ad variations within the same ad group. If AdWords determines that a particular version receives more clicks, it gradually serves it more frequently. Optimize for conversions weights ad delivery in favor of ad variations that provide more conversions. If AdWords doesn't have sufficient conversion data, the rotation is based on the default, optimize for clicks. These options provide easy ways to optimize ads. If you prefer to conduct your own tests, select the rotate option to serve ad variations evenly.

Frequency capping, shown in Figure 5-19, applies to the Google Display Network only. This feature is useful if you prefer to show ads to a greater number of people rather than many times to the same people. The feature limits the number of ad impressions per unique person. The default is no cap on impressions, but AdWords allows limits per day, week, campaign, ad group, or ad.

Figure 5-19. Frequency capping for the Google Display Network

Demographic

The Demographic feature enables exclusion preferences for some websites in the Google Display Network.

If a website collects demographic information and shares it with AdWords (anonymously, of course), it can be excluded based on that demographic. This does not work for the Search Network because age and gender are not required to search. However, people who are members of a social media or dating website probably revealed their age and gender, enabling this feature.

You can exclude by gender or age. For example, if the campaign targets women, use the feature to exclude men, as shown in Figure 5-20. Before doing so, review past performance if data. You might be surprised (or not) to see how different demographics perform.

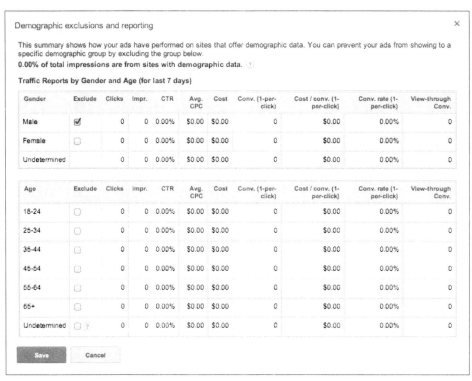

Figure 5-20. Demographic exclusions and reporting

Social Settings

Social settings apply to the Google Display Network, allowing you to specify whether Google's +1 button and annotations appear with ads.

If you're not familiar with Google's +1 button, do a search on Google and look at the results. Next to each result you see a subtle button labeled +1. If you are logged in to a Google account, click the button to endorse a particular search result or websites that include the button on their pages. Your name now appears as a "personal annotation" when your online friends come across the same site. In Figure 5-21, you can see a +1 for the realistic 10-inch opossum sold on Amazon.com (*http://goo.gl/OxEKq*). If Amazon adds the +1 button to its website, the endorsement should appear there, too.

As shown in Figure 5-22, the default is on; to turn it off, click the "Edit" link and select "Do not include the +1 button and the +1 annotations on my ads on the Display Network."

Amazon.com: **Plush Opossum 10": Toys & Games**
www.amazon.com › ... › Stuffed Animals & Plush › Animals & Figures
★★★★★ Rating: 4.7 - 11 reviews - $11.45 - In stock
Eligible for FREE Super Saver Shipping on orders over $25. Details. Product
Description. This realistic 10-inch **opossum** features a long tail, whiskered face, and ...
You +1'd this

Figure 5-21. Use Google's +1 button to endorse websites you like

⊟ Social settings

+1 on Display Network ◉ Include the +1 button and the +1 annotations on my ads on the Display Network.
Display Network only ◯ Do not include the +1 button and the +1 annotations on my ads on the Display
Network.

Figure 5-22. Social settings for the Google Display Network

Inside AdWords (*http://goo.gl/H7UBO*), the official AdWords blog, shows this example
ad in Figure 5-23 to illustrate how ads with social setting appear.

Figure 5-23. Example display ad with new social settings beneath

Keyword Matching Options

If you've used AdWords before, you are probably familiar with keyword match types,
a topic covered in Chapter 6. In May 2012, AdWords changed the way phrase and exact
match keywords are handled. The new default allows ads to trigger on plurals, misspellings, and close variants of phrase and exact match keywords. If you prefer the
previous matching behavior, override the default here. Figure 5-24 shows the new option.

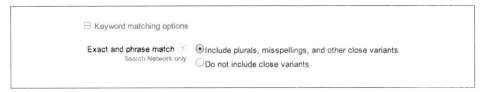

Figure 5-24. Phrase and exact match keyword behavior is controlled in settings

Automatic Campaign Optimization (Display Network only)

Automatic campaign optimization provides access to a tool called the Display Campaign Optimizer (DCO). If enabled, the tool automatically optimizes targets and bids on the Google Display Network to increase conversions.

To use this feature, the campaign must be opted into the Display Network, use Conversion Optimizer with target cost-per-acquisition bidding, and have a minimum of 15 conversions per month.

If you have a hefty monthly budget and many recorded conversions (during beta, the minimum requirement was 150 conversions per month, per campaign), DCO may be a great option. In April 2012, the Inside AdWords blog (*http://goo.gl/NfUBI*) announced that the tool was available to everyone. If you're brand new to advertising, this feature will be something to try after campaigns are set up and recording conversions.

 To learn more about DCO, visit the AdWords Help Center at *http://goo.gl/iuB2i*.

Experiment

The experiment option enables you to easily conduct split tests, testing parts of the campaign against percentages of traffic. Each campaign can run one experiment at a time, with up to 1,000 experimental changes to keywords and bids. Entire ad groups can be set as part of the experiment.

The process is straightforward. First, specify experiment settings. Then, make experimental changes to bids, keywords, and ad groups in the campaign and let it run. As traffic accumulates, check the reports for statistically significant differences. You see the reports under the Campaigns roll-up tab, segmenting by experiment, shown in Figure 5-25 shows the new option.

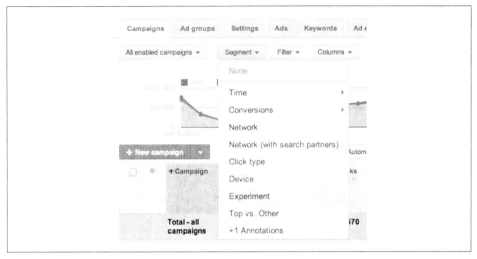

Figure 5-25. View experiment data by selecting the segment

Based on what you learn, apply the changes or remove them.

 For more information about running experiments, visit the AdWords Help Center at *http://goo.gl/VMqvd*.

IP Exclusions

The final advanced feature allows exclusions based on Internet Protocol (IP) addresses. An IP address is a unique string of numbers separated by periods, formatted like this: 123.456.789.12. The address identifies each computer and device connected to the Internet.

By listing IPs, you prevent associated devices from seeing ads. In some cases, a website on the Google Display Network cannot provide a computer's IP address. In this case, ads may receive traffic from excluded IPs.

Figure 5-26 shows the interface. Separate multiple IP addresses with line breaks. You can enter the full IP addresses or use the wildcard character (*) for the last 3 digits to specify address blocks. AdWords allows 100 IP exclusions per campaign.

Figure 5-26. IP address exclusion

CHAPTER 6

Keywords

How Keywords Fit Into the AdWords Auction

Keywords are the basis of the AdWords auction. The auction is a competition between all advertisers who want ads to appear when a searcher types in the keyword or similar words.

AdWords advertisers specify the maximum amount they are willing to pay for an ad click (designated in the account as Max CPC, which stands for *maximum cost-per-click*). With AdWords, winners are not always the highest bidders, because quality is an important factor. The keyword bids and quality combined determine the winners of the auction, as well as the actual cost of individual clicks.

So how do you begin building a keyword list that competes well in the auction and results in profit for your business?

The first thing to keep in mind when building a keyword list is that you cannot force people to search in a particular way. In class, I often ask the group how they learned to search on Google, or if anyone knows how to use advanced operators (*http://goo.gl/ wRuwp*). The vast majority stare with blank faces or shake their heads ruefully. This line of questioning illustrates that the majority of people never learn to search—they simply try words and phrases and look for a hit.

If searchers don't find a relevant result, they try different keyword combinations until they find the results they want. The limitless combinations of search queries makes keyword building a challenge if you want to include every possible way to connect with likely prospects.

Consider why people search Google in the first place; once the probable motivations are identified, keyword research begins and the account is organized accordingly. Let's look at a few reasons why people search and how motivations effect account structure:

A searcher wants to buy something online. He is shopping for the best price, the fastest shipping, the best warranty, the most trustworthy website, etc.

To capitalize on this search behavior, organize accounts by products, focusing on product-centric keywords. The ads should include the keyword and send the searcher to the most relevant product or category pages on the website. For example, an ecommerce website might bid on the keyword `Rush t-shirts` and direct the searcher to a category page featuring every Rush T-shirt style available. If the keyword is more specific, say `Rush 2112 T-shirt`, send the searcher to a specific product page.

A searcher wants to find a brick and mortar location near his location, or near a location he plans to visit.

To help a searcher find the physical location, include location with keywords: `golf in Franklin TN` or `golfing near Franklin TN`. Google uses various geotargeting techniques to display ads on search queries and the searchers' geographic location. Locally focused keywords, combined with features like location extensions and call extensions, help local listings stand out on the search results page. Ad extensions are covered in Chapter 8.

A searcher has a question and wants to find the answer.

To capitalize on this search behavior, use questions as keywords: `how do i make blueberry bush produce fruit?`, `best temperature for snake tank?` The displayed ad should entice the searcher to learn more on the landing page, which should answer the question.

At the very least, this establishes your website as a resource. The searcher may not convert on this visit, but he may return to the site for additional information, return to make a purchase, or refer the website to friends. If you sell fertilizer and supplies for fruit bushes or heaters and equipment for reptile tanks, promote the products on the landing page, alongside the answer to the searcher's question.

A searcher experiences symptoms and wants to identify the problem.

Start by asking yourself how the advertised products or services help solve problems. Searchers use Google to find answers or solutions to issues they experience. Queries like `why does my back hurt when sitting at desk?` or `toes numb elliptical machine` identify problems that need to be solved. If the AdWords campaigns promote ergonomics information, back supports for chairs, or better exercise shoes, include these keywords to connect to searchers who may need your product, but don't know it yet.

A searcher identifies a problem and wants to find a solution.

The searcher has a problem: a family of mice lives inside his Weber grill. Every time he grills burgers, he has to chase them out (and clean up their mess). After the fourth mouse eviction, he searches Google for a solution: `mouse removal`, `mouse extermination`, `how to kill mice`. If you sell ultrasonic mouse deterrents, exterminate rodents, or run a cat adoption organization, this is a great opportunity to display ads.

A searcher wants help with a purchase decision.

A searcher decides to upgrade his ancient television set for a newfangled high-definition model. With so many available options, the query might be: `plasma vs LCD` or `3D TV reviews`, or `top 10 television brands`. Use care when bidding on these keywords because the searcher is in the early stages of the buying cycle, gathering information. But these searches provide an opportunity to develop relationships with potential customers early on.

Organizing Keywords

Once keyword themes have been identified, the next step is to organize them. Each keyword theme becomes a separate ad group. The associated ad text can closely match the keyword theme, increasing relevancy and the likelihood of a click (both increasing Quality Score). In addition, the ad can send searchers to different landing pages that fit the theme.

In theory, an AdWords account can be structured with a one-to-one relationship between each keyword and ad group; hundreds or thousands of keywords make this approach impractical. An easier approach is to monitor traffic at the keyword level; if a particular keyword receives a disproportionate amount of search volume, place it in its own optimized ad group.

Let's look at an example. Someone identified a problem: bald-faced hornets (*Dolichovespula maculata*) created a huge nest under the eaves of his shed. A quick visit to Wikipedia (*http://goo.gl/kW0wZ*): "The bald-faced hornet will aggressively attack with little provocation" and he's convinced that professional services are in order. His next step is to search Google for a local exterminator. A pest control company using AdWords might have an ad group that includes keywords like:

* wasp nest removal
* hornet nest removal
* yellowjacket removal

If this advertiser noticed significant ad traffic on hornet-related keywords, he might remove them from the existing ad group and create a new hornet ad group. Keywords in the new ad group might include:

* hornet nest removal
* bald-faced hornet removal
* hornet exterminator

Now, the ad text can focus on the word "hornet" (ad headline: "We Remove Hornet Nests"). This keyword-focused approach results in a more relevant ad, and typically a higher CTR. Relevancy and CTR result in a higher Quality Score. If the advertiser sends the searcher to a compelling landing page with an easy path to conversion, he can seal the deal: "Bald-faced hornets are more aggressive than yellowjackets and it is not considered safe to approach the nest for observation. Let us remove the nest for you! Book an appointment online or call us at (800) 123-4567!"

Keyword Match Types

Keywords are categorized into two groups: keywords that trigger ads and keywords that prevent ads from showing. New advertisers often neglect the latter, called *negative keywords*. Negatives are a critical component of a successful AdWords account. In some cases, the number of negative keywords exceeds the number of positive keywords in a particular ad group. A thoughtful approach to building a keyword list helps ads show in higher positions, at lower prices, to the most likely prospects. It also prevents ads from displaying on irrelevant searches.

There are different levels of targeting control for both positive and negative keywords. Many new advertisers are unfamiliar with these options, called *match types*. Match types control how closely the keyword must match the search query. By default, keywords are broad match, giving AdWords maximum flexibility to display ads on related queries. Unfortunately, broad match keywords can result in ads being displayed on irrelevant search queries.

For example, the keyword `custom framing` might be used to advertise a business that frames photos and art. But if someone needs a carpenter to frame a new home and searches for `custom home framing`, he might see the picture framer's ad.

Best case, this scenario results in an ad impression without a click. The impression did not cost money, but it did negatively impact clickthrough rate, decreasing Quality Score over time.

Worst-case scenario, the searcher inadvertently clicks on the ad, only to realize the business does not offer the type of framing he needs. A click on the Back button and he's gone, costing the advertiser a click without a conversion. This situation can often be avoided by using keyword match types. Let's review the options.

Broad Match

Broad match is the default match type for keywords. When a word or phrase is added without any special designation, AdWords treats it is as broad. With broad match, AdWords can display ads if the searcher's query matches the keyword exactly, on variations like singular and plural, stemmings, misspellings, as well as related words. These related words are identified by Google's "expanded match technology."

In a nutshell, search queries do not need to match keywords, as long as they are related. Word order does not matter with broad match keywords, and additional words can be included in the search query.

The broad match keyword `custom made shoes`, for example, can trigger ads on search queries like these:

- custom made shoes
- shoes custom-made
- remove shoes for customs?
- origami horseshoe crab pattern

Broad match has pros and cons. On the upside, broad match displays ads on many related queries with minimal effort. One broad match keyword, custom made shoes, can match to a wide range of relevant search queries, like handmade boots, bespoke pumps, pairs of shoes made custom. The same pro is a con if ads are shown on queries like decorative horseshoes, personalized shoelaces, or custom made orthotics. These queries may *seem* related based on expanded match technology, but they may not be relevant to the advertised business.

To prevent ads from showing on irrelevant queries, you must develop corresponding lists of negative keywords to operate as filters. Read on to learn about negative keywords.

Broad Match Modifier

Broad match modifier restricts Google's expanded match capabilities. To use it, select some or all of the words in the keyword you'd like to restrict. Add a plus symbol (+) before each selected word, without a space between. Tagged words must match part of the searcher's query or be a close variant.

For the example keyword +University of +Massachusetts +jobs, acceptable variants include the following:

Obvious misspellings
    University of Massachussetts jobs
Singulars and plurals
    University of Massachusetts job
Abbreviations
    University of Mass jobs
Acronyms
    UMass jobs
Stemmings
    e.g., universities, interuniversity, nonuniversity

The modifier does not allow expanded match to substitute words like careers for jobs, or college for university. Broad match modifier has pros and cons similar to those of standard broad match keywords. Words that are not marked with a plus symbol (+) are treated as standard broad match keywords. Additional words may be included with the search query, and word order does not matter (so Steve Jobs UMass speech can trigger an ad).

Phrase Match

Phrase match can apply to a single-word or multiple-word keyword by enclosing it in quotes (*"keyword"*). Until May 2012, a phrase match keyword had to match the search query, character-for-character, in the same order. The search query could include additional words before and after the keyword. That changed.

Now, the system handles phrase match with more leniency. The phrase must still appear in the query, in that order. But, AdWords will allow ads to trigger on close variants of the keyword, including singular and plural versions, misspellings, and stemmings.

If the phrase match keyword was the single word `silk`, ads could appear on these queries:

- `silk`
- `silks`
- `silk curtains`
- `charmeuse silk wholesale`

If the phrase match keyword included multiple words, for example, `"silk curtain"`, ads could appear on these search queries:

- `silk curtain`
- `silk curtains`
- `silky curtain`
- `silk curtain panels`
- `want to buy silk curtains`
- `buy silky curtains for stage`

Ads *could not* be triggered on these searches, because the phrase is altered:

- `silk for curtain`
- `curtain silk`
- `silk kitchen curtain`
- `silk shade`

Phrase match offers more control in determining which search queries can trigger ads. Because it allows additional words in the search query, it should be used in conjunction with negative keywords to prevent ad impressions on irrelevant queries.

If you prefer the more restrictive version of this match type, override the default in the campaign settings, under Advanced Settings>Keyword Matching Options. This provides more control, but eliminates potentially profitable impressions if misspellings and variations are not explicitly included in the keyword list.

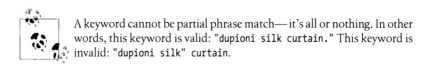 A keyword cannot be partial phrase match—it's all or nothing. In other words, this keyword is valid: "dupioni silk curtain." This keyword is invalid: "dupioni silk" curtain.

Exact Match

Exact match is the most restrictive match type option. It can be applied to a single word or a phrase by enclosing it in square brackets ([*keyword*]). To trigger an ad, the search query must match the keyword exactly. Like phrase match keywords, AdWords now allow ads to trigger on close variants of exact match keyword, including singular and plural versions, misspellings, and stemmings. Unlike phrase match, no other words can appear in the query.

For example, if the exact match keyword is [broadway plays], ads can trigger on the search query: broadway plays and close variants in the same word order, like:

- broadway play
- braodway play
- braodway plays

Ads *cannot* trigger on any other query, no matter how close:

- broadway shows
- nyc plays
- play broadway

Like phrase match, an exact keyword cannot be a partial match—it's all or nothing. This keyword is valid: [broadway plays]. This keyword is invalid: [broadway] plays.

From the pro perspective, exact match gives you absolute control over which queries trigger ads. Negative keywords are unnecessary, because queries must match exactly. And you will likely receive high marks for relevancy, since the search query and keywords are identical. On the con side, the restrictive nature of the match type eliminates potentially profitable ad impressions if you do not include all variations.

Negative Keywords

Negative keywords operate as filters, preventing ads from triggering on search queries that contain them. A negative keyword is a single word or a phrase, prefaced by a single minus symbol (-*keyword*). Like positive keywords, negatives have different match type options. Let's start with the default, simply called "negative keywords."

If the negative keyword is a single word, for example, -rent, ads cannot trigger on this search query: cabin for rent.

Unlike with positive broad match keywords, there is no expanded match technology applied for negatives. To prevent your ads from showing on irrelevant queries, all variations of a negative keyword must be included:

- `-rents`
- `-rental`
- `-rentals`
- `-renter`
- `-renting`
- `-renters`

If the negative keyword includes more than one word, the filter only works if *all* words appear in the search query. The words can appear in any order, but they must match character-for-character. For example, the negative keyword `-black pearl` prevents ads from triggering on these queries:

- `black pearl replica`
- `black tahitian pearl`
- `pearl black touch-up paint`

It does *not* prevent ads from triggering on these example queries:

- `black ship replica`
- `black tahitian pearls`
- `pearly black paint`

Negative Phrase-Matched Keywords

Negative phrase-matched keywords combine the minus symbol and quotes: (`-"phrase in here"`). These keywords prevent ads from appearing when multiple words appear in a specific order in a searcher's query. For example, the negative phrase-matched keyword `-"black pearl"` does prevent ads from triggering on these queries:

- `necklace black pearl`
- `black pearl model ship`

It does *not* prevent ads from triggering on these example queries:

- `black model ship`
- `black tahitian pearls`
- `pearl jewelry`

Negative Exact-Matched Keywords

Negative exact-matched keywords combine the minus symbol and square brackets: (-
`[word or phrase in here]`). These keywords prevent ads from appearing when a search
query matches the negative keyword exactly. The search query cannot include any
additional characters or words, the words must be in the same order, and the characters
must match exactly. So, the negative exact-matched keyword `-[black pearl]` prevents
ads from showing only on the search query `black pearl`. It does not work for `pearl
black`, `black pearl necklace`, or any other variation.

This particular match type is useful for virtually every advertiser because some keywords are too generic (or have too many different meanings) to be profitable. Excluding
them as standard or phrase-matched negative keywords could prevent ads from
appearing on relevant search queries, but a negative exact-matched keyword fits the
bill. Here are a few examples:

- A jeweler sells Tahitian pearl jewelry. He discovers that most searches for `black
  pearl` do not convert (perhaps searchers are looking for Captain Jack Sparrow's
  ship). This AdWords account might benefit from the exact-matched negative keyword `-[black pearl]`.

- A bridal boutique notices a spike in AdWords traffic without corresponding conversions. The advertiser excludes `-[Bridesmaids]`, because searches for the popular
  movie may be resulting in irrelevant impressions and ad clicks.

- A wholesale distributor of fine silk excludes the keyword `-[silk]`; the keyword has
  too many other meanings (soy milk, restaurants, salons, the R&B group, etc.) to
  assume the searcher is a likely prospect. Some prospects may be lost, but the overall
  cost savings outweighs the lost impressions.

Which Match Types Are Best?

There is no specific formula for using keyword match types; to some extent it depends
on the preference of the advertiser. Some ad groups include a single broad match keyword, with many, perhaps hundreds, of negative keywords. Other ad groups include
only exact match keywords, in many iterations.

Although Google officially discourages this approach, many advertisers include the
same keyword in all three match types within the same ad group. In this scenario,
queries that match the keyword are credited to the exact match version; queries that
include additional words are credited to the phrase match version, and broad match is
the catch-all.

Use this technique to assign higher bids to more specific match types (based on the
assumption these queries are more likely to convert). The disadvantage of this approach
is that managing the account can become unwieldy with so many keywords to deal

with. Your account is not penalized for including all three match types, and keywords in the same ad group do not compete against each other.

Keyword Rules and Editorial Guidelines

There are several rules to keep in mind when creating keyword lists. This section provides tips that apply to all keywords.

A keyword is a keyword, not an AdWord.
>	AdWords is the brand name of Google's advertising platform.

A keyword is a single word or a phrase.
>	Keywords are limited to 80 characters and cannot contain more than 10 words.

Keywords are not case-sensitive.
>	The keyword `JELLYCAT BASHFUL BUNNY` is the same as `jellycat bashful bunny` and `Jellycat Bashful Bunny`.

Most symbols are not allowed in keywords.
>	The following characters result in an error if included when adding a keyword: ! @ % ^ * () = {} ; ~ ` <> ? \ |. Ampersands (&) are allowed in keywords.

Periods, commas, and hyphens are treated as spaces.
>	For example, if the keyword is `www.example.com`, AdWords treats it as three separate words: `www example com`. One exception to this rule is apostrophes that indicate possession.

Diacritics (accent marks) are treated as unique characters.
>	For example, the keyword `resume` is not the same as `resumé`. Include all variations in your keyword list.

You are responsible for selected keywords, and in most countries AdWords does not restrict the choice of keywords.
>	In effect, you can include competitors' trademarked terms in a keyword list. The rules vary by country (*http://goo.gl/RXHnh*); in most regions Google does not disable an account or keyword if a trademarked term is used as a keyword. As of the writing of this book, AdWords allows U.S.-based advertisers to include trademarked terms as keywords. Ad text is another story—in most cases, you are not allowed to use competitors' terms in ads. This is not legal advice, so please chat with an attorney if you have any questions.

How to Manage Keywords

To manage keywords in your AdWords account, start on the Campaigns tab. Then, select the campaign and ad group from the tree view. Click the Keywords roll-up tab from the middle pane. There are two places to manage keywords in this view. At the top you manage keywords that trigger ads. At the bottom, under the link labeled Negative Keywords, you manage negative keywords, which prevent ads from displaying.

To add keywords to an empty ad group, click the button labeled "+Add keywords" (shown in Figure 6-1); to add additional keywords to an ad group, click the "+Add keywords" button (shown in Figure 6-2).

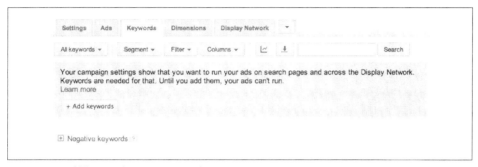

Figure 6-1. Add keywords to an empty ad group

Figure 6-2. Add additional keywords to an ad group

AdWords may display additional keyword ideas, shown in the box in Figure 6-3. Manually type or paste new keywords or add keyword suggestions from the right column.

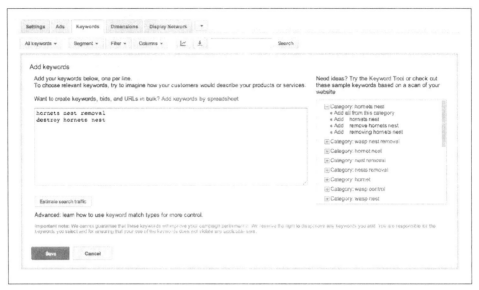

Figure 6-3. Type or copy and paste keywords into the box; additional suggestions appear in the right column

There are two ways to edit existing keywords, via inline editing and via Google Spreadsheets. To use inline editing, click the keyword, make changes directly in the row, and save. Before edits are made, AdWords displays the rather menacing warning box shown in Figure 6-4.

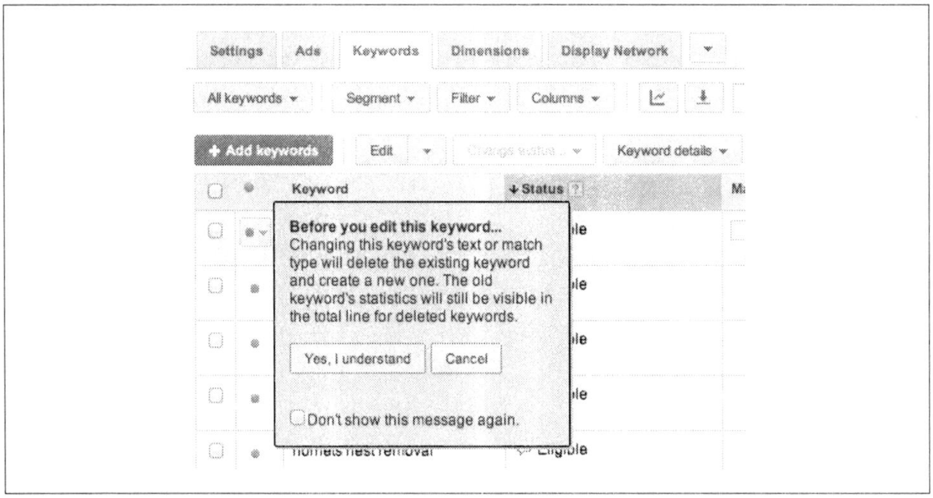

Figure 6-4. A dire warning

The warning means that if keyword text or match type are edited, AdWords treats the keyword as new. Visible statistics for the keyword are reset to zero. This does not mean that AdWords erases the history of the keyword's performance in the account. To keep the visible statistics, pause the keyword and create a new keyword with the desired changes. Edit a single keyword by clicking it. Edit multiple keywords inline by selecting checkboxes and clicking Edit → "Edit in table." See Figure 6-5.

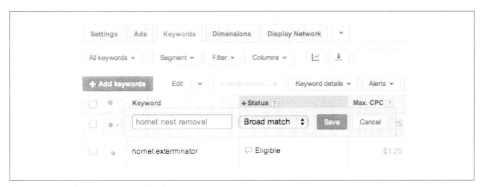

Figure 6-5. Editing a keyword inline

Editing with Google Spreadsheets

The second option is editing with Google Spreadsheets (shown in Figure 6-6). Spreadsheets offer an additional handy feature: the ability to set destination URLs at the keyword level. Keyword-level URLs override the matched ad's destination URL. The feature is useful if a particular keyword has a more relevant landing page than the default matched ad. Rather than create a new ad group, use keyword-level destination URLs to send searchers to the best landing page.

For example, an ad group for the removal of stinging insects includes keywords like `yellowjackets`, `wasps`, and `hornets`. The destination URL specified in the ad text sends searchers to a page about the removal of all stinging insects.

If there is a better destination URL for a particular keyword, set it here rather than create another ad group.

Settings | Ads | Keywords | Dimensions | Display Network | ▼

Spreadsheet edit

Use Google Spreadsheets to add, edit, delete, or pause your keywords. You can also set or edit unique keyword bids and Destination URLs   Learn more

	A	B	C	D	E	F	G
1	Keyword	Status	Max. CPC	Destination URL	First Page CPC	Clicks	Impressions
2	hornet nest removal	enabled	$1.25		$0.35	0	0
3	hornet exterminator	enabled	$1.25		$0.01	0	0
4	remove hornets	enabled	$1.75		$1.75	0	0
5	hornets nest removal	enabled	$1.50		$1.5	0	0
6	destroy hornets nest	enabled	$1.25		$0.7	0	0
7	how to remove hornets	enabled	$1.25		$2	0	0

Figure 6-6. Edit keywords with Google Spreadsheets

Keyword Status

Keywords have three status options: Enabled, Paused, or Deleted. To toggle between enabled or paused, click the green dot shown in Figure 6-7 (enabled) or gray paused icon (paused).

Figure 6-7. Pause or enable keywords

To delete a keyword, you must select the corresponding checkbox, click the "Change status" button, and select Deleted (see Figure 6-8).

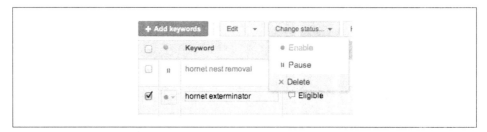

Figure 6-8. Delete keywords

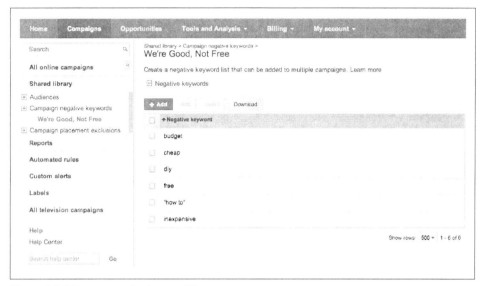

Figure 6-9. Manage negative keyword lists

Managing Negative Keywords

Negative keywords are managed separately, in a section at the bottom of the page. Note that there are two types of negative keywords: ad group level and campaign level. Ad group–level keywords apply to the corresponding ad group; campaign-level keywords apply to all ad groups within the campaign.

To add negative keywords, click the "+Add" button and type or paste words in. To edit a negative keyword, click it for inline editing. To edit multiple negative keywords, select checkboxes and click Edit or Delete.

The same options are available for campaign-level negative keywords, plus an additional feature called *keyword lists*. A keyword list is a campaign-level exclusion list created and managed from the "Shared library" section of the account, found under the tree view.

You can save negative keyword lists and use them for multiple campaigns. This makes account management more efficient, because updates happen at the list level, not for individual campaigns or ad groups (Figure 6-9).

Keyword Details Reports

One of the handiest features in an AdWords account, labeled "Keyword Details," is found under the Keywords roll-up tab. It's useful because it identifies the search query—the actual words typed into Google by the searcher—that resulted in an ad click. Unfortunately, the report does not identify search queries that result in impressions without clicks, but it's still a great place to start optimizing a keyword list.

Use this report to find out if the search queries make sense. Let's say you sell high-end event supplies, using keywords like:

- `dome tent`
- `canopies`
- `banquet tables`

With broad match keywords, similar search queries can trigger ads. But what if a similar word or phrase, or the nuance of a word or phrase, is irrelevant to your business? In most cases, clicks on irrelevant search queries result in a wasted click. In this example, the report shows you paid for clicks when ads where shown on these queries:

- `coleman 4-person dome tent`
- `tree canopy zipline tour`
- `rent banquet tables`

If you do not sell camping tents, operate zipline tours, or rent equipment, these clicks most likely did not result in a sale. When you run the report, ask yourself, *did each search query make sense for the business?* If yes, add the query to the keyword list (if it's not there already). For irrelevant queries add to the negative keyword list.

Be sure to review the conversions column—it's possible that a seemingly irrelevant keyword is generating conversions, too. The interface—albeit clunky—allows you to do just this. View search queries for an individual keyword, a set of keywords, or all keywords. Let's review an example report, shown in Figure 6-10.

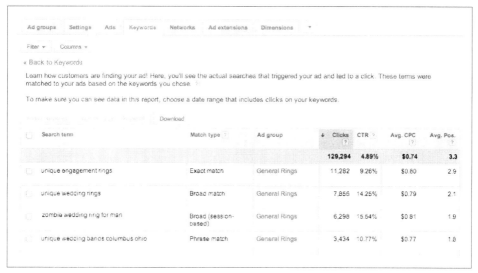

Figure 6-10. The "Search terms" report

The first column, labeled "Search term," shows the search query that triggered an ad. The second column, labeled "Match type," reports how closely the search query matched a keyword. This is *not* the same as the match type of the keyword that triggered the ad. If the value is "Broad match," it means that query does not appear in the keyword list, but AdWords triggered the ad because it's a related term. If the match type is "Phrase match," it means the search query matches part of a keyword. "Exact match" means the search query matches the keyword exactly (even if the keyword is broad or phrase match). The last value, "Broad (session based)," means the search query is a variation of a keyword, and ads were triggered based on previous searches by the same person during that session. Table 6-1 shows a few examples.

Table 6-1. Understanding the search query report's "Match type" column

Search Query	Corresponding Keyword	Match Type in Report	Why?
custom designer wedding rings	unique custom made rings	Broad	The search query is a variation of the keyword. It applies to broad match keywords only.
unique rings for couples	unique rings	Phrase	The search query contains the keyword. It does not matter if the keyword is broad or phrase match.
custom unique engagement rings	custom unique engagement rings	Exact	The search query matches the keyword. It does not matter if the keyword is broad, phrase, or exact match.
engagement rings without diamonds	unique engagement rings	Broad (session-based)	Various search queries from the searcher's session are related to a keyword in the ad group.

Now, its time to review the actual queries. Row-by-row, examine the search query and ask, *Does this makes sense? Was it relevant?* If you have conversion tracking set up for the account, review conversion statistics per keyword. Add relevant keywords by checking the corresponding boxes and clicking the button labeled "Add as keyword." Now, do the opposite. Check the boxes associated with irrelevant keywords and click the button labeled "Add as negative keyword," shown in Figure 6-11.

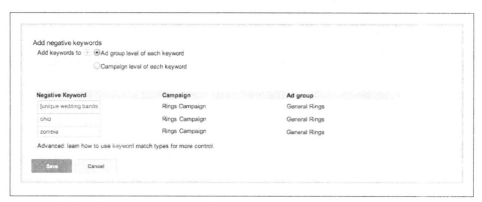

Figure 6-11. Identify irrelevant search queries

The next step is to save the word or phrase as a negative keyword in an ad group, campaign or negative keyword list in the shared library. Note that AdWords puts the entire search query in as an exact negative match by default. I often edit the search query so the filter is less restrictive. For example, if you decide to create a negative keyword from the search query unique wedding bands columbus ohio, the system default is to put this entire phrase in as an exact match. This filters a single query: those exact words, in that order. It does not filter a search for columbus ohio unique wedding bands. If the irrelevant words are "Columbus" and "Ohio," edit the keyword to make the filter more effective, adding negative ohio and columbus. You may need to add/edit several times to get all the combinations you want. Remember, ohio is not the same keyword as oh, and columbus is not the same as colombus.

If you save the entire search query as-is, it will be labeled "Excluded" in red (see Figure 6-12). If you edit the search query before saving it as a negative, it omits the red flag, but it's still saved.

 Another small annoyance: after saving, checkboxes beside rows do not automatically deselect. Remember to deselect before working on additional rows.

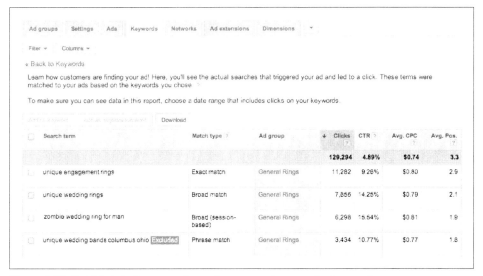

Figure 6-12. Red labels indicate search queries are saved as negative keywords

If you see search queries labeled broad, phrase, or broad session-based, they do not appear exactly as keywords in your account. You can use this report to add them to the account (which should increase the Quality Score for future matching queries). Again, select the appropriate queries, and then click the button labeled "Add as keyword." The entire search query appears, with a default broad match type. Edit the search query or change match types as desired, then click Save. If the search query exceeds 10 words or 80 characters, it must be shortened before being saved; otherwise, it displays an error that prevents saving any checked rows.

If you've never reviewed this report on an active account, there may be hundreds or thousands of rows to review. Work on this project in manageable chunks, perhaps 100 rows at a time, back to the beginning of the account history. Then, run the report on a regular basis to see recent activity and make updates to the keyword list (see Figure 6-13).

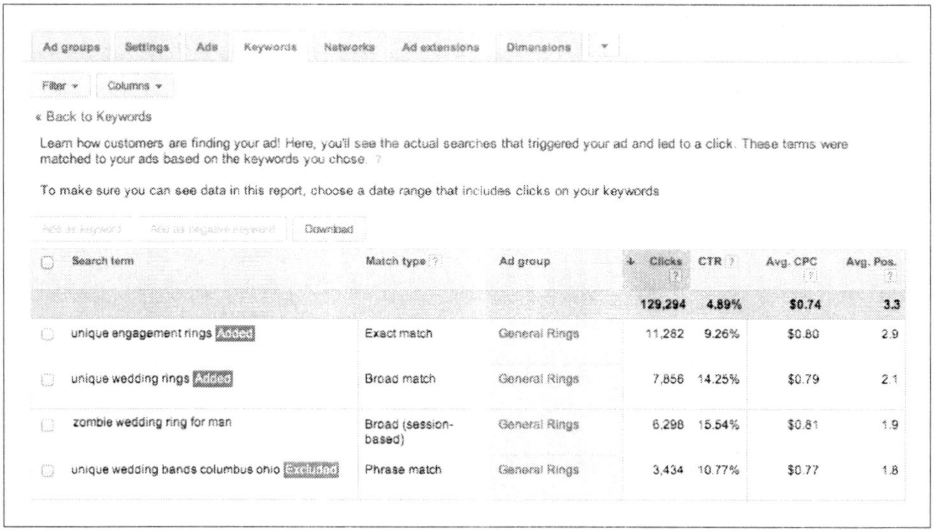

Figure 6-13. A search query report with keywords added and excluded

The second report under Keyword Details is called "Auction Insights." Unlike Search Terms, this report is for a single keyword. But, it shows how your keyword compares to specific competitors in terms of impression share, average position, plus overlap rate. The report shows a list of the domains included in the competitors' ads. The report shown in Figure 6-14 indicates that five advertisers surpass this advertiser in terms of impression share, but overall the keyword is extremely competitive.

How to Use the Keyword Tool

One of the most popular keyword research tools in the search marketing industry is free and built into every AdWords account: the Keyword Tool. You can access this feature from the "Tools and Analysis" tab in the top navigation. The keyword tool is useful for identifying keywords to include and exclude from the account.

Start by entering a word, phrase, or website with relevant keywords, and then click Search. The report displays up to 800 related keywords to consider (100 ideas for a website). You can refine results in several ways. To restrict results to ideas that include the original search terms, check the box labeled "Only show ideas closely related to my search terms." You can add filters, displaying ideas for specific countries and languages, adult ideas, devices, and categories like search volume, competition, and approximate CPC.

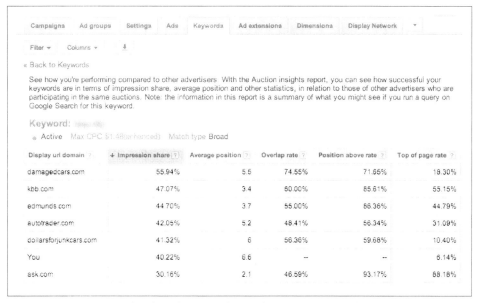

Figure 6-14. Auction insights shows how your keyword stacks up against the competition

The report shows ideas by row, with associated information. Competition does not show the raw number of advertisers competing on the keyword, but gives you an idea of how competitive the keyword is in comparison to its search volume. Local Monthly Search Volume shows the average number of search queries in the last year, based on specified location.

Review the list for keywords to add. You can select multiple rows, but all selections must be saved into a single ad group. Work in stages, selecting themed keywords and saving them in batches to the appropriate ad groups. Alternatively, create a draft ad group with a paused status. Then, save all keywords into this draft group for future organization. Another option: select rows, and then download the report. Open in Excel or Numbers and add to ad groups later.

In this example, the seed keyword ring shows 800 ideas. If you're working on a jeweler's account you can find relevant keywords like engagement ring. You can also identify irrelevant keywords, like free ring tones and ring worm. Many advertisers neglect negative keyword lists; this tool is handy for eliminating lines of search behavior you may not have considered.

To add negatives, click the downward-facing arrow next to the keyword (Figure 6-15) and select "Exclude term." From here, you can view a search results page, view an Insights for Search report or use the keyword as a new seed keyword.

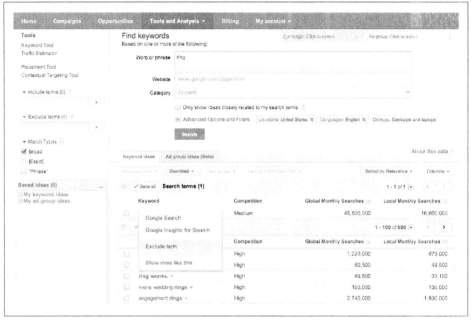

Figure 6-15. Use the Keyword Tool to identify positive and negative keywords

A new addition to the tool is the ad groups suggestion tab. Now the seed keyword results in a list of possible ad groups and associated keywords. Add the ad groups and some or all of the keywords by clicking the "Add to account" button.

Using Google Insights for Search

Google offers a free, external tool designed for advertisers and researchers called Insights for Search (*http://goo.gl/JbGXF*), shown in Figure 6-16. Insights compares search volume patterns across specific regions, categories, time frames, and Google properties (Products, Images, News, and Web). The tool shares the same data as Google Trends (*http://goo.gl/W5RxL*), but the interface facilitates research beneficial to AdWords advertisers.

For example, you can use Insights to research the popularity and seasonal fluctuations of particular search queries. A comparison of the terms "south beach diet," "weight watchers," and "atkins diet" reveals an unsurprising surge in related searches every January. The tool also reveals smaller, yet regular spikes in search volume every April or May and September. Use this information to make sure campaigns have appropriate conversion incentives and budgets during peak search times.

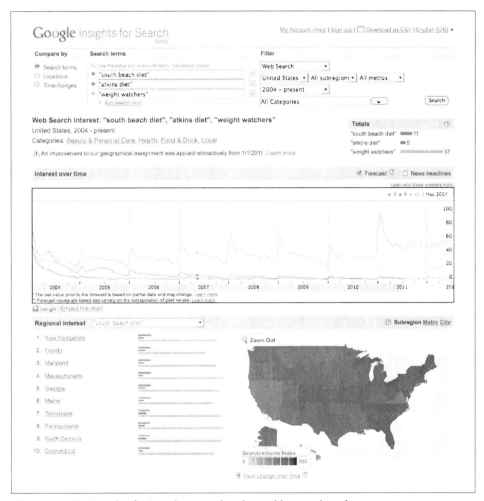

Figure 6-16. Use Insights for Search to see what the world is searching for

Insights displays activity back to 2004 as well as a forecast of future traffic. View data for different countries, subregions, and metros, and in 40+ languages. Compare the popularity of a search term with others, and see a list of "rising searches," searches with significant growth during the viewed time period.

Insights may also display a Breakout section to highlight queries with 500 percent growth or higher. Insights does not provide raw search volume numbers, but instead a graph representing popularity on a scale from 0–100.

Another neat feature: enabling "News headlines" shows headlines from the selected time period, as shown in Figure 6-17. This provides insight into the fluctuations shown in the report. Click the letter labels to see the corresponding news stories in the right column.

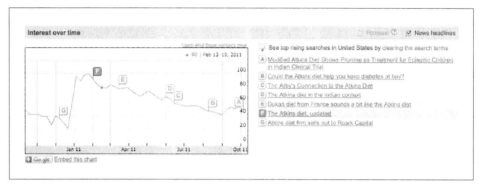

Figure 6-17. Use Insights to see news headlines during traffic fluctuations

CHAPTER 7

Writing Ads

Ad Text Requirements

For many AdWords advertisers, writing ads is the least favorite account management activity. Yet ad text is critically important. The searcher is looking for an answer to a question, a solution to a problem, a way to fulfill a need or desire. If you've got what the searcher needs, the ad text is your opportunity to convince him to visit the website.

It's difficult to present a compelling case for your product or service within the meager 130 character limit (95 if you don't count the Display URL). You not only compete against other AdWords advertisers, you compete against the organic results, and sometimes local business results (Google Places or Google+ Local). On a crowded search results page with many options, your ad needs to set you apart and convince the searcher that your website has what he's searching for.

This chapter reviews technical and editorial specifications, and then provides tips for writing and testing ad variations.

AdWords text ads include four distinct lines. The first line is the headline or title of the ad. It allows up to 25 characters, including spaces. The next two lines, called Description Line 1 and Description Line 2, allow up to 35 characters each, including spaces. The fourth line, called the Display URL, allows up to 35 characters. There is one additional field to complete, the Destination URL. This specifies where an ad click "lands" on the website; sometimes this page is called the landing page.

Ad text specifications

Headline	25 characters maximum, including spaces
Description Line 1	35 characters maximum, including spaces
Description Line 2	35 characters maximum, including spaces
Display URL	35 characters maximum
Destination URL	1,024 characters maximum

An ad looks like this:

```
This is the Headline
This is Description Line One.
This is Description Line Two.
www.this-is-the-display-url.com
```

And sometimes like this:

```
This is the Headline
www.this-is-the-display-url.com
This is Description Line One.
This is Description Line Two.
```

Ads that appear in the yellow box above the organic search results, called *top ads* or *top-ranked ads*, may have a slightly different presentation. Instead of four distinct lines, Description Line 1 may appear with the headline, separated by a hyphen. AdWords does this if each line appears to be a distinct sentence and ends in proper punctuation. In other cases, the display URL appears with the headline. As a result, some top placement ads have longer headlines.

Top ad variations look like this:

```
This is the Headline - This is Description Line One.
www. this-is-the-display-url.com
This is Description Line Two.
```

Or like this:

```
This is the Headline - www. this-is-the-display-url.com
This is Description Line One.
This is Description Line Two.
```

Let's review some ad formatting and style rules.

- *You cannot skip lines.* All five lines of your ad text must have a value.
- Ad must be written with *proper spacing.* Your ad may not be approved if you omit spaces or add extra spaces or characters between words. These examples violate Google's guidelines:

```
CallUsToday!
Call  Us  Today!
Call--Us--Today!
```

- *Punctuation and symbols* must be used properly in a sentence in the ads, not as a way to attract attention or replace words. AdWords does not allow repeated punctuation, and it limits exclamation points to one per ad (and only in the description lines, not in the headline or Display URL). "Texting" language is not allowed, so "2 Hot 4 U" won't fly.
- AdWords does not allow ad text with unnecessary *repetition.* "Sale Sale Sale" doesn't pass.

- Ads must use *proper capitalization*. You cannot write an ad with all uppercase letters (although all lowercase may pass). You are allowed to capitalize the first letter of each word, if you wish. These examples pass Google's guidelines:

  ```
  30% Off All Summer Clothes!
  30% off all summer clothes!
  ```

  These examples violate Google's guidelines:

  ```
  30% OFF ALL SUMMER CLOTHES!
  30% off ALL summer clothes!
  ```

- The Display URL is subject to additional rules. First of all, AdWords does not display *http://* or *https://* in ad text, so these characters do not count toward the 35 character limit. The *www.* is optional; if you choose to include it, the four characters do count toward the character limit. If the Display URL is longer than 35 characters, it's truncated. For example, if the Display URL is *www.mydogsarenamedmissyjasmineandparis.com*, it is displayed as *www.myarenamedmissyjasmineandpa...com*.

  The Display URL must be a website and the Destination URL must be an HTML page. It doesn't matter what the file extension is (*.htm*, *.html*, *.asp*, *.php*, *.jsp*; any will do). You cannot display or link to an email address or a non-HTML file (PDF, MS Word, JPG, etc.).

  The domain of the Display URL must match the domain of the landing page URL. You are permitted to use a redirect, like a URL shortener, as long as the final destination domain matches the displayed domain. In other words, if you advertise a website, you must send visitors there, not to a different site. This applies to subdomains as well; you cannot advertise *flowers.example.com* and send visitors to *www.example.com*. However, you can use the Display URL *example.com* and send visitors to *flowers.example.com*. Some advertisers circumvent this rule by using redirects; even if the ad is approved initially, it may be disapproved eventually.

  While the domain must be accurate, anything that follows does not! In other words, you can add words or phrases after the Display URL's domain name. This may improve the relevancy of your ad, even if the additional words don't represent actual web pages or directories. You might add keywords, or the location, or a phone number to help the ad stand out or be more relevant to the search query.

  For example, if you are advertising for a pet supply store in Buffalo, New York, your Display URLs might look like this:

  ```
  www.example.com/Buffalo-NY
  example.com/800-123-4567
  example.com/Pet-Supply-Store
  example.com/We-Carry-Orijen
  ```

  The Destination URL does not need to match the displayed URLs. Select any page within the displayed website; the URL character limit is 1,024 characters. One caveat: if a searcher decides, for whatever reason, to copy and paste or manually type the Display URL, and it's not a real page, this may result in a "Page Not Found" or 404 page. So, if a searcher sees this ad:

```
Premium Dog Food
Buffalo's Premier Pet Supply Store
Open 7 Days, Come In and See Us!
example.com/Pet-Supply-Store
```

And if he manually types in the Display URL, *example.com/Pet-Supply-Store*, he sees a page like Figure 7-1.

Figure 7-1. Google's 404 or "page not found" error page

Yuck.

Your options are: create a friendly 404 page with navigation and a search box to help visitors find what they are looking for; automatically redirect 404s to a real page, like the homepage; or (best scenario) set up redirects so displayed URLs redirect to the corresponding destination URLs.

One final note about Display URLs: AdWords automatically displays the root domain (everything from the *www.* to the domain extension) in lowercase when ads are displayed on Google. Even if the ad is written with caps, *Example.com*, searchers see *example.com*. However, if you include additional words or characters after the root domain, AdWords does allow capitalization. Here are a few examples of ways Display URLs may appear on Google search results pages:

```
www.example.com
example.com
example.com/More-Words
example.com/more-words
example.com/MoreWords
```

This rule does not apply to ads shown on the Search Partners or the Google Display Network; there, your Display URL capitalization is typically preserved in the visible ad.

Advertising in Asia? You are probably using double-byte characters

If you are advertising in a language such as Chinese, Korean, Japanese, or other East Asian languages, you're probably using double-byte characters. Double-byte characters use almost twice the amount of display space as single-byte characters, so the limits are different. The headline has a 12-character maximum; the description lines and display URL have a 17-character limit. For ASCII symbols, like punctuation marks, and alphanumeric characters (the numbers 0–9 and letters A–Z), use single-byte characters. If your AdWords interface is set to display in a single-byte language, like English, the displayed character limits are incorrect. Manually count characters to comply with the double-byte limit.

AdWords Ad Policies

Along with technical requirements, ads are subject to an extensive list of editorial guidelines. Most are common sense, but it's a good idea to review the policies before running ads. It's best not to get on "the list" of accounts with frequent ad policy violations. If an ad violates a policy, it's labeled "disapproved" and cannot be displayed. Once you correct the issue and resubmit the ad, it is eligible to participate. However, if Google determines that a violation is an extreme policy breach, or if your ads are repeatedly disapproved, Google can suspend the account or ban you from AdWords.

Occasionally you see an ad that violates one or more editorial policies. The ad probably slipped through the automated quality control. AdWords uses a human team to manually review ads, and eventually the ads may be disapproved. Let's review guidelines that impact most advertisers.

 See the most up-to-date rules in the AdWords Policy Center: *http://goo .gl/8UVMO*.

Rules About Ad Content

Don't mislead people

AdWords requires ad text to accurately represent the content on the landing page. If a searcher looking for "wooden children's toys" clicks on an ad for "Handmade Wood Toys," the landing page should present the expected products. If the landing page promotes something different, say, an ebook about parenting skills, the ad may be disapproved. The policy requires that ads and landing pages display real, accurate information about the advertiser.

Be polite

Don't swear or self-censor (F*ck, *sshole, sh*t) in ad text.

Support competitive claims

Don't say you are better than a competitor unless your landing page clearly explains why. This might be a chart comparing products or services or a competitive analysis.

Support superlative claims

Don't say you're the best unless someone else has said so (and this does not include customer testimonials or praise from your mother). If you use a superlative claim in your ad, a credible third party must be cited on the landing page. For example, if your business was voted a "Best of Nashville" winner in the local newspaper's reader poll, your ad can use that verbiage. The landing page must include a reference to the award and preferably a link to the referenced claim.

Avoid generic calls to action

AdWords does not allow calls to action that could apply to any ad, regardless of content. For example, generic phrases like "click here," "visit the website," and "select this ad" don't pass. Examples of acceptable ad verbiage include "buy now," "order today," "learn more," "browse our catalog," and "preview 2012 styles."

You can use phone numbers

You can display a phone number in your ad, with two exceptions: not in the headline or in a sitelinks extension.

Some topics are limited or off-limits

AdWords restricts some topics, including abortion, sexual services, alcohol, casinos and gambling, drugs and drug paraphernalia, endangered species, counterfeit documents, fireworks, hacking, health care and medicines, illegal products and services, solicitation of funds, tobacco products, trade sanctions and restricted parties, traffic devices, underage and nonconsensual sexual acts, and weapons. There are various nuances to these topics. For example, you cannot advertise hard alcohol, but it is permissible to advertise beer, wine, and champagne. Refer to the Restricted Products and Services (*http://goo.gl/3FSe3*) section within the AdWords Policy Center to get information about each topic.

Prices, discounts, and offers

The AdWords policy states that if an ad promotes a price, discount, or offer, it must be found within two clicks of the landing page. For free offers, you're not required to explicitly say "free," but it should be obvious to the site visitor. To avoid approval issues, I recommend putting this information on the landing page. This may also improve your conversion rate, since the searcher presumably expects to find that offer after reading your ad. If you use the words "guarantee" or "warranty" in your ad, AdWords requires that you provide the details and any major limitations.

Pleas for popularity
Your ads can't encourage or incentivize searchers to click the Google +1 button.

Rules About Ad Functionality

Malware (malicious software)
You cannot promote software that steals, spams, commits fraud, disrupts usage, or the like. Malicious or not, you cannot trick people into installing software.

Deception
You cannot promote products or services that mislead people for financial gain. AdWords also prohibits deceptive practices like phishing.

Personal information security
You must use secure servers when collecting personal or financial information. In addition, you must clearly disclose when you do this and request permission from visitors. Sites collecting payment or financial information must disclose prices and billing practices in an easy-to-understand way. Permission must be obtained before processing payments.

Ad spam
You cannot promote exploitation for financial gain. Examples include artificial ad traffic; pay-to-read, pay-to-surf, and pay-to-click programs; traffic exchange programs; pyramid schemes; and claims of a special relationship with Google.

Arbitrage
You cannot advertise websites designed to persuade visitors to click more ads.

Bridge or doorway pages
You cannot promote *bridge pages* that send visitors to a different site. Bridge pages are sometimes used to comply with AdWords policies; the page sends visitors to a different website with non-compliant content. Affiliate websites with minimal content may also be considered bridge pages.

Mirroring and framing
You cannot promote websites that use techniques known as *mirroring* and *framing*. Mirroring refers to websites with multiple copies across servers or domains. Framing refers to the use of HTML framesets to display the information from one website within another website.

Parked domains
You cannot promote parked domains or websites under construction. These sites typically present a list of related links and ads unrelated to the search.

How to Create and Edit Ads

Ads are associated with ad groups, and thus tied to the keywords and placements within that ad group. When you create a new campaign or a new ad group, the setup wizard includes a "Create an ad" section, shown in Figure 7-2.

Figure 7-2. Write an ad in a new ad group

New text ad

Write your text ad below. Remember to be clear and specific. Help me write a great text ad.

Headline
Description line 1
Description line 2
Display URL
Destination URL   http://

Ad preview: The following ad previews may be formatted slightly differently from what is shown to users. Learn more

Side ad
New York Budget Hotel
Clean and close to subway
Students save 20%!
www.example.com

Top ad
New York Budget Hotel - Clean and close to subway.
Students save 20%!
www.example.com

Ad extensions expand your ad with additional information like a business address or product images. Take a tour!

Character limits for ads targeting Eastern European and Asian countries. All enabled and paused ads are subject to review.

Save ad   Cancel

Figure 7-3. Write an ad in an existing ad group

To create or edit ads for existing campaigns and ad groups, start by selecting the desired ad group from the tree view. Then, navigate to the Ads roll-up tab. From there, click the "+New ad" button and select "Text ad" from the drop-down menu (shown in Figure 7-3).

Now, edit or rewrite the ad displayed in the edit space (shown in Figure 7-4). You can see a preview of the new ad on the right side. When you're satisfied, click "Save ad."

You can also edit existing ads. Start by moving your mouse to the top right corner of the ad. Look for the pencil icon (shown in Figure 7-4).

When you click the pencil, the warning box shown in Figure 7-5 appears: "Before you edit this ad... Changing the ad deletes the existing ad and create a new one, which will be submitted for review. The original ad's statistics will still be visible in the total line for deleted ads." You must click the "Yes, I understand" button before proceeding.

Many advertisers stop at this point, worried about losing valuable information. Here's the deal: If you want to keep the original version of the ad and its associated statistics,

Figure 7-4. Edit an existing ad

Figure 7-5. Editing an ad deletes the existing ad. The visible stats for the revised ad are reset to zero, but you can find the old ad's statistics in the total line for deleted ads.

don't edit. Pause it and create a new ad. If you don't need the original version with its data, edit the existing ad. Either way, historical data is included in the "totals" row. However, the edited ad is considered new, and its statistics reset to zero.

How to Write Powerful Ads

Effective ads are clear, simple, and relevant. You have a very small amount of space, 130 characters (including the Display URL), to convince a searcher to click your ad and learn more. With so many other websites vying for the searcher's attention, how can you help your ad stand out in a crowd?

First of all, stay on topic The ads you write should closely reflect the theme of the keywords or placements in the ad group. For example, if the ad group is focused on custom-made purses, the ad text should, too. AdWords does not usually work well when generic ads are displayed for specific searches. If you can present the searcher's query (or something close to it) in the text of the ad, you have a greater chance of winning the click.

When you write an ad, consider the two ways you'll sell it: benefits and features. What's the difference? Benefits tug at the searcher's heartstrings, convincing him that the ad provides the solution to a problem, fulfills a need, or delivers happiness (whatever that may be for the searcher). Strong ads often open with benefits, to connect with the searcher and convince him to learn more.

Features describe the "nuts and bolts" aspects of the offer. That might be free shipping, or a money-back guarantee. Use features to help close the decision process for the searcher, to convince him to use your company.

Ideas to Try

Call to action
>This is perhaps the easiest way to increase clickthrough rate and conversion rate. If you tell the searcher what's supposed to happen after an ad click, you'll increase the likelihood that she does it. Ironically enough, AdWords does not allow the verb "click." Even though in most cases all a searcher will do is click on an ad to learn more, the call to action must use another word, like "Buy Chocolate for Mother's Day," "Order Holiday Hams Today," or "Download a 30-Day Trial."

Different capitalization
>AdWords does not allow excessive capitalization in ad text, but it does allow ads to be rendered with uppercase and lowercase letters. Compare these ads:

>```
>Jasmine's Nursery
>We Sell What Organic Gardens Need.
>Plants, Seeds & Supplies - Buy Now!
>example.com
>```

>and

>```
>Jasmine's Nursery
>We sell what organic gardens need.
>Plants, seeds & supplies - buy now!
>example.com
>```

>Without testing, it's impossible to tell which capitalization style will prove more effective for the advertiser. Each ad group allows multiple versions of ad creative. You can create two variations to test which results in a higher clickthrough rate (and conversion rate, once conversion tracking is set up).

Different Display URLs
>The Display URL is a factor in the AdWords Quality Score calculation. The algorithm tracks whether particular variations are stronger than others. In 2011, AdWords changed how Display URLs are shown on Google Search results pages. Prior to the change, ads could show a Display URL like this:

>```
>ExampleWebsite.com
>```

Now all characters in the root domain are displayed as lowercase, no matter how they are written in the AdWords account. So, in the example above, the searcher would see:

```
examplewebsite.com
```

You have the option to append additional text after the display URL. Interestingly enough, this text does *not* have to represent a real web page or directory, nor does Google lowercase it. If you are advertising for a nursery, the Display URL could be:

```
example.com/Lavender-Plants
```

AdWords automatically changes *example.com* to lowercase, but any subsequent words will follow the capitalization convention you specify.

Different conversion incentives
These include offers, coupons, and discounts. Conversion incentives are a critical way to convince searchers to learn more about your company. It's a good idea to review what competitors are saying in their ads on important keywords. Now think, *How can I make my ad different and more compelling? What can I provide that will convince a searcher to pursue my business rather than my competitors?*

Contrasting conversion incentives include: convenience versus shipping costs, free returns versus money-back guarantee, 25 percent off versus $50 coupon.

Experiment with different conversion incentives to see which perform best in various markets. You may find that an ad that performs well in one metro may flop in another. You may find that conversion incentives for rural searchers varies from those for searchers in metro areas. The ability to add multiple ad variations to a single ad group enables testing ad variations. You should continually test ad variations because subtle differences can have a huge impact on ROI.

Try numbers
Numbers often work well in ad text. Experiment with text like "Top 10 Tips" or "50 Style Ideas."

Try prices
Prices can serve two purposes. If you sell a product at a competitive price, test ad copy with the price included. This technique can work if the searcher is truly cost-conscious and your prices are lower than competitors. But what about the opposite scenario? If you are selling a high-end product or service, publishing the price may discourage clicks from consumers searching for lower-cost items. In this scenario, you can add negative keywords that operate as budget qualifiers, keywords like `cheap`, `inexpensive`, and `low-cost`.

You should run ongoing tests as long as you use AdWords. It takes a minute to create a second variation, and the algorithm can help determine which variation is the strongest performer.

How to Use Dynamic Keyword Insertion

Dynamic keyword insertion (DKI), sometimes referred to as "wild card," is an ad text trick that can make an ad seem more relevant to a searcher by inserting the keyword into the ad text. So who uses this, and why?

Let's assume you have a website that sells cable and wire. You have tens of thousands of products in various categories, including coaxial cable, computer cable, industrial cable, fire alarm cable, and the like. Each of these categories has subcategories, with products identified by codes. To include the keyword in the ad text, you'd have to create a separate ad group for each product. With the sheer number of products, it's impractical to create a separate ad group for each individual product. But DKI makes this manageable.

To set it up, you place a piece of code in the ad text. This tag can be placed in any or all lines of the ad text. When someone searches Google for one of the keywords in your ad group, the tag is replaced by the keyword that triggered the ad. The tag looks like this:

```
{Keyword:The Default Text}
```

Let's go over the elements of the tag.

The body of the tag is enclosed by curly brackets: { }

Within the curly brackets, include the word "Keyword." The capitalization of this word determines how the ad renders to the searcher.

keyword
> all words appear in lowercase.

Keyword
> The first letter of the first word is capitalized. all others are lowercase.

keyWord
> the First Word Is Lowercase. For Additional Words, The First Letter Of Each Word Is Capitalized.

KeyWord
> The First Letter Of Each Word Is Capitalized.

KEYWORD
> ALL LETTERS ARE CAPITALIZED.

KEYword
> THE first word appears in all capitals

KeyWORD
> The FIRST WORD STARTS WITH A CAPITAL. ALL ADDITIONAL WORDS APPEAR IN ALL CAPS.

KEYWord
> THE First Word Appears In All Caps. For Additional Words, The First Letter Of Each Word Is Capitalized.

If you use DKI to make ads text appear in uppercase, violating editorial guidelines, ads will be disapproved eventually.

 A note on match type and dynamic keyword insertion. If the keywords in the ad group are broad match, AdWords can trigger an ad based on related terms, but it displays the bid term, not the search query. So, if your ad group contains the broad match keyword `marine wire`, and a searcher types in `cable television for houseboat`, that may trigger the ad, but the ad text will say "Marine Wire" because that keyword triggered the ad.

After "Keyword" comes a colon (:). There are no spaces before or after the colon.

After the colon follows the default text. The default text is a backup, in case the keyword that triggered the ad does not fit into the character limits. For example, if the keyword triggering the ad is "High Voltage Coaxial Cable," it exceeds the 25 character limit for the ad title. In this situation, AdWords shows the ad, but substitutes the default text for the bid term. The default text must adhere to the AdWords character limits; the only word you cannot use is "default."

Let's go back to our cable and wire example. In the AdWords account, you create an ad group promoting high voltage coaxial cable. Within this subcategory, there are 50 different cable products. Rather than create an ad group for each individual product, you use DKI to insert the product code for each type of cable in the headline of the ad.

Some of the keywords in this ad group might look like this:

- R5743-1
- R5234-1
- 2R1032-4
- R1006-1

You want to use dynamic keyword insertion to insert this keyword into the title of the ad. Your tag looks something like this: `{KEYWORD:High Voltage Coax Cable}`. You use this tag as the title line in your text ad. Dynamic keyword insertion replaces the tag with the bid term.

Written out in the account, your ad looks like:

```
{KEYWORD:High Voltage Coax Cable}
All Types of High Voltage Coaxial
No Minimum Order, Ships Today!
example.com
```

Now, let's assume a searcher's query was `R5743-1`. If you won a place in the auction, the searcher sees this ad:

```
R5743-1
All Types of High Voltage Coaxial
```

```
No Minimum Order, Ships Today!
example.com
```

If the search query was R5234-1, the searcher sees this ad:

```
R5234-1
All Types of High Voltage Coaxial
No Minimum Order, Ships Today!
example.com
```

DKI can apply to all lines, including the destination URL. For the biggest advantage, work with your developer to set up redirects that send searchers directly to the product pages associated with keywords. So, if your destination URL was:

```
http://www.example.com/products/{KEYWORD:High-Voltage-Coax-Cable}
```

And it rendered as:

```
http://www.example.com/products/R5234-1
```

It should send the searcher directly to the corresponding product page on the website. Next-best scenario: send the searcher to the category page for that set of keywords. But, as with everything in AdWords, the more specific you are, and the easier you make it for the searcher to convert, the more successful the campaign will be.

Be careful when creating keyword lists using DKI. You must be sure that the rendered text reads well and makes sense. Have you ever noticed ads that don't make any sense? The text might say something like "Save on Buy Live Chickens" or "All About Buy Live Chickens." It's a good bet a human did not write that ad; it's probably sloppy DKI work.

A worse scenario: the ad makes sense but it's (accidentally) offensive. If your store sells high-end toys, the ad headline might read "Buy {KEY-WORD:Toys for Babies}." The keyword list presumably includes all the names of the toys. But what if the keyword list included words like babies, infants, kids and, children? Now, the ad says "Buy Babies" or "Buy Infants." Yuck. Use your imagination to come up with the million ways to stick your foot in your proverbial mouth.

CHAPTER 8

Making Ads Stand Out

Ad Extensions

There are up to eleven AdWords ads on a page. Lucky advertisers have few competitors, but for most, at least some keywords cause ten competing ads to appear on the search results page. In this situation, the challenge is not only to win a desirable position on the page but to make the ad noticeable and compelling. Higher position on the page often helps improve clickthrough rate, but relevancy is a huge factor. Even if the ad appears in the last position on that page, it has a chance of winning the click if it's the most relevant result for the searcher.

Optimizing ads begins with proper account organization. If the ad group is focused on a specific theme, the ad text can reflect that theme. But what happens if all your competitors do this well, too? How can you make your ad stand out? An AdWords feature called ad extensions lets you do just that.

Extensions are "add-ons" that make ads appear more relevant or useful for a searcher. They can also occupy a larger area on the search results page. There is no additional cost for using extensions, but if the extension connects a searcher with the advertiser, the advertiser is charged for a click. You can implement multiple extensions for each campaign, but not all extensions are applicable for every situation.

There are six types of ad extensions: location, sitelinks, products, social, mobile app, and call. You may not see all extensions in your account.

Extensions are available at the campaign level. I wish they were available at the ad group level; until that happens, adjust your account organization to associate different extensions with specific ad groups. Ad extensions are created and managed in two places. For new campaigns, ad extensions are set up with the campaign settings, as shown in Figure 8-1.

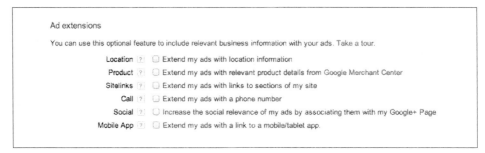

Figure 8-1. Ad extensions appear in settings for a new campaign

For existing campaigns, ad extensions are managed from an optional roll-up tab labeled "Ad extensions." If you do not see it, click the arrow symbol to the right of the roll-up tabs to display the menu of optional tabs, shown in Figure 8-2. Check the box labeled "Ad extensions" and the roll-up tab becomes visible in the account.

Figure 8-2. Ad extensions for an existing campaign

Within the "Ad extensions" roll-up tab, the navigation is subtle. See Figure 8-3. In the top left corner you see a gray area labeled "View: [Extension Name]." Click this box to see the menu of extensions and select the option you want to manage.

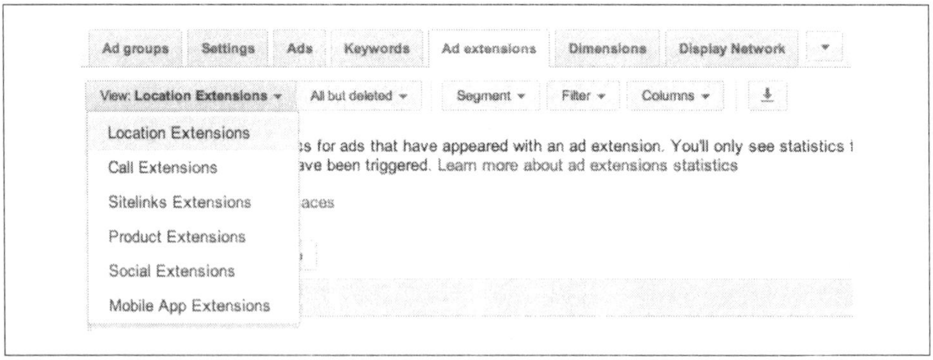

Figure 8-3. Selecting extension categories to manage

Let's review each ad extension in more detail.

Location Extensions

A location extension improves a text ad by displaying the business address beneath, as well as a link to directions from Google Maps. Figure 8-4 shows an example. Occasionally the search results page displays a map below the ad, usually for top-ranked ads. To set up location extensions, manually enter an address or connect the AdWords account with a Google Places account.

 On May 30, 2012, Google rolled out Google+ Local (*http://goo.gl/ 1GOHV*), which integrated business listings with the Google+ social platform. Places pages were automatically migrated into the Google+ Local format. It's assumed that at some point Google Places will be entirely replaced with Google+ Local. As of this writing, the AdWords interface derives location extension data from Google Places listings.

Location extensions can appear on ads in Google Search and some sites in the Search Partners and Display Network, on both computers and mobile devices. Location extensions are extremely helpful for local businesses with brick and mortar locations. If you operate a web-based business or if customers do not visit your location, you will not use this extension.

Figure 8-4. Example ad with location extension

So, how do you set this up? Start by creating a Google Places account, preferably using the same login as AdWords. Google Places (*http://www.google.com/places/*) is a free business directory. Results are displayed on Google.com and other properties, including Google Maps. Many businesses already appear in the Places directory without any work; the directory was pre-populated with data from other sources. Business owners can create a new listing or claim an existing listing. Once the business listing is claimed, associate the listing with an AdWords account to display business details with ads.

For a new campaign, specify the location extension with the campaign settings. Under the "Ad Extensions" section, check the box that says "Extend my ads with location information." Select "Use addresses from a Google Places account" to connect to your Google Places account. If the Places account login is the same as the AdWords account, you do not need to enter the password; it automatically connects, as shown in Figure 8-5.

Figure 8-5. Connecting to a Google Places account

If you are associating the AdWords account with a different email address, you need the password, too. Businesses have the option to specify an icon from the AdWords library or upload a custom icon to accompany the listing. Icons should be 16 × 16; *.gif*, *.png*, and *.jpg* formats are accepted.

If you do not have a Google Places account, manually enter an address, add an icon, and add a business image (Figure 8-6).

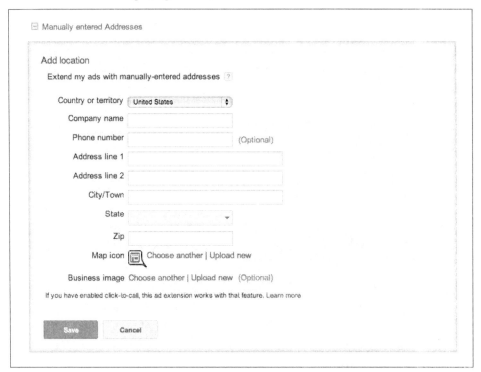

Figure 8-6. Manually enter a location extension

If a searcher requests directions from the link below an AdWords ad, the advertiser is charged the same price as a click.

If your Google Places account includes multiple locations, AdWords automatically selects the closest location to the searcher's physical location or search intent.

Location Extensions Versus AdWords Express

You may notice ads that have a blue pin icon, address, phone number, and directions link below (see Figure 8-7).

Figure 8-7. AdWords Express ad (top ranked)

Many of these ads are not created via location extensions, but with a simplified version of AdWords called AdWords Express. Formerly known as Boost, it offers an easy entry into AdWords.

Here's how it works. Businesses create or claim a Places Page or a Google+ Local page. Next, they setup an AdWords Express account at www.google.com/awexpress (*http://goo.gl/UzBvT*).

Once an account is created, the system asks for business details and descriptive categories. Next, write ads and specify where a click takes the searcher (either their website or a Google+ Local page). See Figure 8-8.

Then, a budget is selected. Unlike AdWords, AdWords Express operates on a monthly budget. The minimum budget varies by category; the lowest amount is $50 USD per month, per category. Like AdWords, it uses a cost-per-click model so you are charged only for clicks.

Once set up, AdWords Express automatically creates ad groups, keywords, and bids, and runs the ads.

AdWords Express is a fit for small, local businesses, showing ads to searchers in a 15 mile radius around the business address. If your business needs to show ads beyond a 15 mile radius, you need to use the standard AdWords platform.

A few additional things to note. AdWords Express is very simple to use, but you sacrifice control. You cannot set maximum bids or change any part of the ad group besides the ad creative. You can review AdWords Express campaigns in your AdWords account, but you cannot edit them there (see Figure 8-8). From the AdWords Express account you can edit ad text, categories, and budget, but all other advertising decisions are handled automatically by the software.

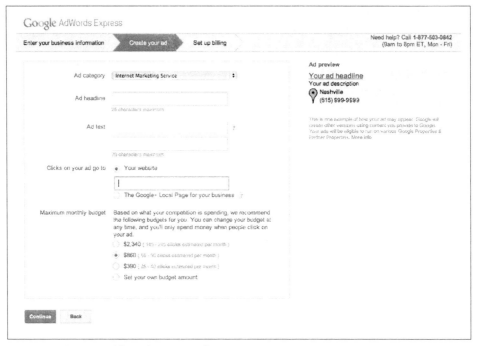

Figure 8-8. Create an AdWords Express ad

Figure 8-9. AdWords Express campaigns in AdWords user interface, labeled "Places Ads_xxxxxxx"

 You can use an AdWords Express account to get a jump start on account structure in a standard account. First, create a campaign using AdWords Express (make sure it's associated with a standard AdWords account, too). Then, open the standard account in AdWords Editor. From here, you can see the AdWords Express campaigns. Create duplicate campaigns, copying the AdWords Express campaigns. Now you can edit them as standard campaigns. Then turn off AdWords Express to complete the switch.

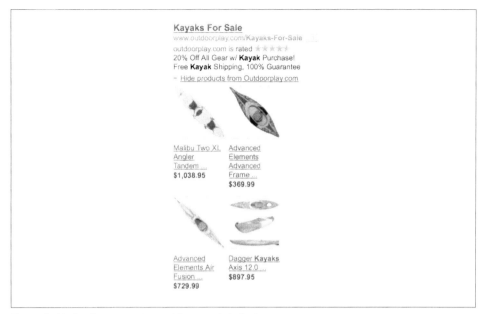

Figure 8-10. Product extensions with expanded plusbox

Product Extensions

If you have an ecommerce site, product extensions allow you to display product images with AdWords ads. To do this, you must have a Google Merchant Center (*http://www .google.com/merchants/*) account and feed products into it. The Merchant Center account is free; use it to upload products into Google's Shopping database. Connecting AdWords with the Merchant Center is simple if the login emails match; otherwise, you need to provide the username and password. Product extensions appear on Google Search only, on all devices.

The extension appears as a set of thumbnail images below the ad text, including the title and price of the product.

Product extensions may be shown in plusbox format, visible when the searcher clicks the plus symbol to view associated products (see Figure 8-10). You are not charged when the plusbox is expanded, only when a product is clicked. As with most extensions, the price for a product thumbnail click corresponds to an ad click.

To select products to display, the AdWords system compares the searcher's query to product attributes. If it can match attributes to the search query, the product may appear beneath an AdWords ad. To help AdWords identify appropriate products, you must include specific attributes with each product in the Merchant Center feed. The minimum attribute requirements are as follows:

condition [condition]

The condition of the item. There are three accepted options: new, refurbished, and used. New products must be brand-new and in original, unopened packaging. Refurbished products must be restored to working order. "Used" applies to everything else, including products whose original packaging has been opened.

description [description]

The description identifies the product. It can be up to 10,000 characters, but the recommended length is 500–1,000 characters. The description should be very specific to the product and not include special offers or information about the seller.

id [id]

A unique identifier for each product in the Merchant Center account. Use any sequence of numbers and letters. The sequence must be unique, even across multiple feeds.

link [link]

The URL of the product page on the website. A searcher lands on this URL when the item is clicked as a product extension or in Google's Product Search. The landing page cannot require a username or password, have pop-ups or pop-unders, or be a direct link to a file or email address.

image link [image_link]

A URL of a product image. Do not submit a thumbnail image; the recommended minimum image is 400 × 400 pixels. Apparel images must be 250 × 250 pixels or larger. Placeholder images, brand logos, and store logos are not acceptable.

price [price]

The product price.

title [title]

The title of the item. It should include brand, product name, characteristics (size, color, etc.), and category. The title is limited to 70 characters.

The {adtype} valuetrack parameter separates clicks from product listing ads and product extensions. To set this up, edit the product's click-through URL in the Merchant Center account to track how a visitor got to the website.

{Adtype} is replaced with a value showing which ad type a visitor saw. For example, if a product listing ad is clicked, the URL:

www.example.com/product.php?origin={adtype}

is replaced with:

www.example.com/product.php?origin=pla

If a product extension is clicked, the URL is replaced with:

www.example.com/product.php?origin=pe

Sitelinks

Sitelinks are one of the simplest ways every advertiser can improve ads. A standard text ad offers a single landing page option, associated with the headline and the display URL. Using sitelinks, you can display two, four or six additional display URLs below the ad.

Sitelinks promote additional areas of the website, as well as drive special promotions and reinforce conversion incentives.

Figure 8-11 shows an example ad with sitelinks. Sitelinks are displayed for top-ranked ads only. Each sitelink includes a display URL (up to 35 characters) and a destination URL (up to 1,024 characters). The user interface allows up to ten sitelinks to be associated with each campaign, but the search results page displays a maximum of six. If you upload more sitelinks than available placements, AdWords will select randomly from the options.

Figure 8-11. Sitelinks example

Clicks on sitelinks cost the same as clicks on the ad headline or display URL. You can create a separate set of sitelinks for each campaign or share a single set across multiple campaigns. If you edit the shared set, all campaigns are updated.

There are three types of sitelinks:

Two and three-line format
> shown when the ad offers an ideal answer based on the search query, usually triggered on brand terms.

One-line format
> shown on generic terms, occasionally brand terms.

Embedded format
> links appear in ad text, no additional lines appear below ad. Will appear when ads don't meet the requirements for other sitelink formats.

Embedded sitelinks appear when the ad doesn't quality for additional lines, but the text in the sitelink Display URL exactly matches text in the ad. For example, if the ad reads:

Beekeeper Equipment
We Sell Everything Your Bees Need.

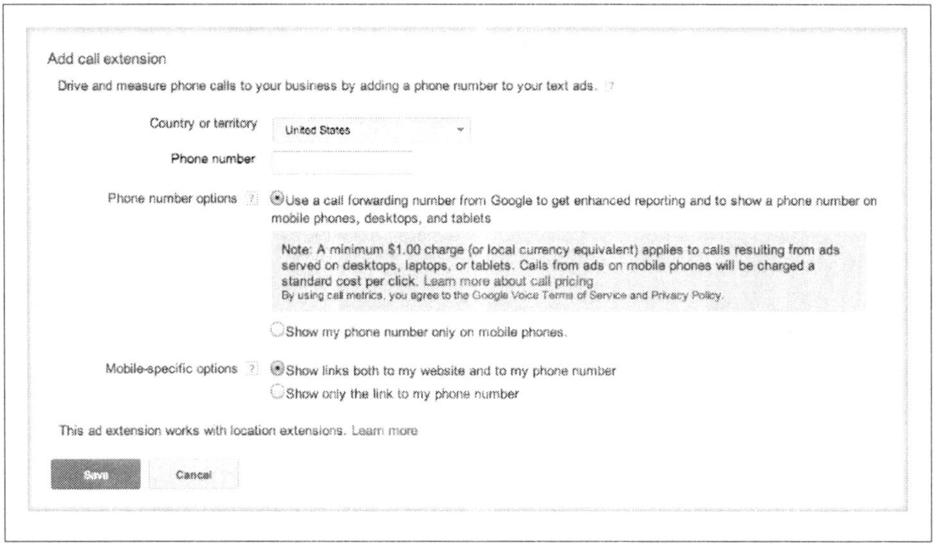

Figure 8-12. Call extensions

```
Bee Suits, Veils & More. Buy Now!
example.com
```

And the campaign includes the following Sitelinks:

- Display URL: Bee Suits; Destination URL: *http://www.example.com/bee-suits.php*
- Display URL: Veils; Destination URL: *http://www.example.com/bee-veils.php*

AdWords embeds the links in the text of the ad. There are no additional lines. To embed links, some text in the ad (Description Line 1 or 2) must exactly match the sitelink Display URL. In this example, the ad looks like this:

```
Beekeeper Equipment
We Sell Everything Your Bees Need.
Bee Suits, Veils & More. Buy Now!
example.com
```

Call Extensions

Call extensions (also known as click-to-call) allow you to associate a trackable phone number with text ads. AdWords offers two options: call-only and Call Metrics (United States and U.K. only). Figure 8-12 shows the interface.

Call-only applies to ads on mobile devices using CPC bidding. With this extension, the destination URL is replaced by a clickable phone number. Instead of sending visitors to a website, a click triggers a phone call to a number specified by the advertiser. If a searcher sees the an ad on a desktop or laptop computer, the extension will not appear.

You can use most types of phone numbers, including local, toll-free, shared-cost, and vanity phone numbers (e.g., 877-ADWORDS instead of 877-239-6737). A call from the ad is the same price as an ad click. It can appear on tablet computers like iPads, but a click on the phone number sends the visitor to the landing page, since the device isn't a phone!

AdWords displays the number of impressions, clicks (calls), average CPC, cost, and average position for ads with the call-only format (Figure 8-13).

Figure 8-13. Call-only format

Call Metrics applies to all devices. Using Google Voice technology, Call Metrics displays a unique phone number that forwards calls to a number specified by the advertiser. Caller ID works even though the phone call is routed through Google.

Unlike other extensions, pricing is set at $1 USD per phone call. You can bid more by specifying a maximum CPP. The Max CPP bid and "phone call Quality Score" factors into Ad Rank, too. Phone call Quality Score is a separate calculation from Quality Score for clicks. The most important factor is historical phone-through rate (the number of phone calls received divided by the number of times the phone number is displayed).

The actual CPP is calculated similarly to click pricing, with an additional averaging step. For each ad auction, Google calculates a cost-per-call for every advertiser. This cost is influenced by bids and Quality Score (clicks and calls), relative to other ads. Google then averages the calculated call costs over the last few auctions to determine actual call cost. Bid-per-call does not apply to ads on mobile devices, which use a cost-per-click model. In a nutshell, the higher the CPP and CPC bids, the more likely the ad is to win the auction.

You are charged for redialed or manually dialed calls for 48 hours after the number is displayed with an ad. The number is not yours to keep; Google may eventually reassign or discontinue it.

Call activity currently does not factor into ad rank or Quality Score. To see activity reports, visit the Dimensions roll-up tab to see start time, end time, status (missed or received), duration, cost, and area code (see Figure 8-14).

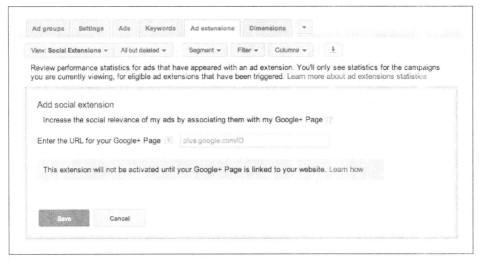

Figure 8-15. Social extensions

↓ Start time	End time	Status	Duration (seconds)	Caller area code	Phone cost	Call type
Jun 16, 2012 6:35:36 PM	Jun 16, 2012 6:35:52 PM	Received	16	412	$0.00	Mobile click-to-call
Jun 15, 2012 6:00:10 PM	Jun 15, 2012 6:00:25 PM	Received	15	706	$0.00	Manually dialed
Jun 15, 2012 5:58:03 PM	Jun 15, 2012 5:58:10 PM	Received	7	706	$0.00	Manually dialed
Jun 14, 2012 5:53:46 PM	Jun 14, 2012 5:53:57 PM	Received	11	918	$0.00	Mobile click-to-call
Jun 12, 2012 4:45:30 PM	Jun 12, 2012 4:47:10 PM	Received	100	310	$0.00	Mobile click-to-call

Figure 8-14. Reports from the Dimensions roll-up tab

Social Extensions

A social extension (Figure 8-15) connects an AdWords account with a Google+ Page. By default, AdWords ads have an associated +1 button. Clicking this +1 button is an endorsement of the business. With social extensions, if someone clicks the +1 button on your website, the endorsement appears with your AdWords ad, and vice versa.

One requirement: your Google+ Page must be connected with your website. Google uses this information to determine the relevancy of the website to search queries.

To learn more about connecting a website with a Google+ Page, visit the AdWords Help Center: *http://goo.gl/lBnCo*.

Figure 8-16. Mobile App extensions

Mobile App Extensions

The mobile app extension (Figure 8-16) is for a very specific set of advertisers: those promoting mobile apps sold in Google Play or the Apple App Store.

Like other ad extensions, it appends more information to text ads. In this case, you can add a link to the mobile app in an app store, in hopes of increasing downloads. Unlike sitelinks, which offer multiple links to pages on your site, only one mobile app extension displays per text ad. Once enabled, customers can click through to the website from the ad headline or click through to the app store.

CHAPTER 9

The Google Display Network

Introduction to the GDN

Google Search works splendidly when a searcher knows what she wants. Her search query identifies what she wants to find, so you have a chance to present your offers on the search results page. But what about the searcher who wants what you sell but doesn't know it yet? You might have the greatest product in the world, but if the searcher doesn't know it exists, how can she find it?

Or what if your product is extremely visual? A searcher might pass by a text ad, but an image or video has a much greater chance of catching her eye.

Enter the Google Display Network. This network is made up of millions of "placements," locations where AdWords ads are eligible to appear. Placements are websites, online games, web feeds, and online video sites like YouTube. Ads are contextually targeted. In other words, you specify keywords or themes (called *topics*) and the AdWords system identifies relevant placements to show the corresponding ads. You can hand-pick placements, called *managed placements*. Unlike Google Search, the Display Network offers many ad formats, including text, image, Flash, and video ads.

If the differences between Search and Display are not yet clear, consider this scenario.

A searcher visits Google because her pet bearded dragon has outgrown its terrarium. After researching options, she searches for "Exo Terra PT 2613" to find sellers. In this case, the search query identified what she wanted at that moment in time. An AdWords advertiser selling the terrarium has an opportunity to make an immediate sale.

Compare this to someone visiting a bearded dragon forum, reading up on dietary information for her baby dragon. In this situation, the visitor may not need a new terrarium. But what about six months from now? As the dragon grows bigger, so do the housing needs. If the pet owner has seen ads for Exo Terra terrariums for the last six months, the ads might influence her research and decision process.

That being said, the GDN offers tremendous reach and significant ad exposure beyond search. AdWords has steadily introduced new tools and features to help understand performance and make refinements. For new advertisers, I generally recommend that the GDN be tabled until Search campaigns are running smoothly. When you are ready to run a Display campaign, set it up with care. Create a separate campaign. Monitor ad spend, performance on placements, and conversions. This chapter provides a brief introduction to advertising on the Display Network; the topic is so large it merits a separate book.

The Display Network Tab

Showing ads on the Google Display Network is called an ad distribution preference. This preference is set in the campaign's settings but the actual management happens in the Display Network roll-up tab (previously labeled "Networks").

The Display Network tab is composed of four sections: Display Keywords, Placements, Topics and Interests & Remarketing. Let's cover them.

Display Keywords

A recent improvement: AdWords now provides keyword-level performance statistics for the Display Network. You'll see it in the Display Keywords area, which shows performance and conversion data keyword-by-keyword. If the campaign is opted into both Search and the GDN, keywords cannot be edited here (visit the Keywords roll-up tab to make changes). If the campaign is limited to the Display Network you can edit keywords from this area.

The Display Keywords section highlights major differences between search and display. For one thing, the keyword list should be much shorter than a search keyword list. By limiting the number of keywords to 5-10 words on the GDN, you can focus on a particular theme. Unlike search, all GDN keywords are broad match, so variations, plurals, misspellings and other variants are unnecessary. Limiting the number of keywords, helps the target placements relevant to the core theme of the ad group.

With the improved reporting, you can review which keywords are high and low performers on the GDN, and make adjustments accordingly.

Placements

The Placements area looks like the old Networks tab, providing performance statistics for managed placements: placements specified by the advertiser; automatic placements: placements selected by AdWords; and exclusions: a list of placements where ads cannot appear.

For both automatic and managed placements, you can see a URL list, which shows a link to every page where ads were shown on the Display Network. You can use this list to refine placements. For example, you might want to show ads on a particular site,

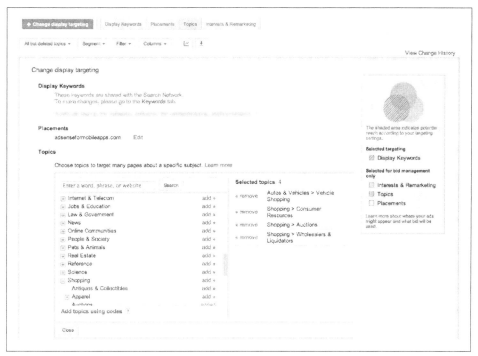

Figure 9-1. *Select relevant topics to expand reach on the Display Network*

but exclude specific pages or directories. By reviewing the list, you see performance statistics that show you what's working and what's not.

If you cannot decide which placements are appropriate for your campaign, one strategy is to use the automatic placement option, at least for a period of time. With automatic placements, AdWords selects placements to show ads. AdWords uses the theme and the keywords to find appropriate placements.

As AdWords displays ads on placements in the network, you see the results reported in the Automatic Placements section. Review performance; if a placement is relevant and performing well, you may decide to add it to the managed placements list. If a placement is not performing well, consider adding it to the exclusions list.

Topics

Once a separate roll-up tab, Topics provides a way to expand your reach by targeting web pages relevant to selected topics. This targeting method allows ads to appear on any pages that have content related to selected topics. Topic targeting can be used in combination with placements and keyword targeting. Figure 9-1 shows how adding a topic expands the advertising reach.

By targeting the "Autos Vehicles > Vehicle Shopping" topic, ads can appear on any placement with automotive sales themes.

Interests & Remarketing

The Display Network roll-up tab holds another useful AdWords feature, called *remarketing*.

Here's how it works. A person visits your website, including a page tagged with remarketing code. This person may or may not have searched Google or clicked on an ad. All you know is that the person visited a web page and a cookie was placed on his computer. This person is added to a group of people who did the same thing, defined as an audience in the AdWords account.

Enter remarketing. If AdWords knows that a particular computer is part of an audience, it can show ads on pages in the Google Display Network, based on audience membership. Think of remarketing as a reminder that follows your website visitors around the Internet. From an advertiser perspective, remarketing is a dream come true; the trick is to not scare people away.

Audience lists are defined in the Audience section of the Shared Library, found in the tree view. Think of each audience as a group of prospects (people who visited products A–G, people who signed up for an email newsletter, etc.).

To enable remarketing, a piece of code is embedded on the target page of the website. This code tells AdWords to save these visitors to an audience list you created. When people visit a tagged page, their cookie ID is added to a corresponding remarketing list. Once the remarketing tag is in place, ads target people on the lists while they browse other websites. Remarketing ads are not shown to people who are not on the audience list.

Remarketing can be set up intelligently. You can define audiences to target and audiences to exclude (for example, people who converted). For example, you might set up a remarketing list for an ecommerce website. You want to show ads to people who came, but did not buy. To do this, create a second remarketing list recording visits to the purchase confirmation page (the "Thank You" page).

Then, create a custom combination, showing ads to people who visited, minus those who converted. Custom combinations and interest categories can define specific audiences in "and," "or," or "not" relationships.

 Learn more about interest-based advertising and audiences at the Ad-Words Help Center: *http://goo.gl/aUyU*.

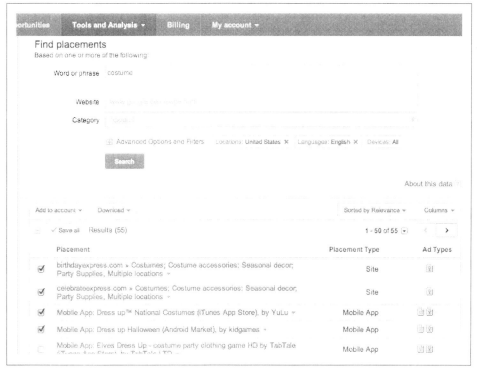

Figure 9-2. The Placement Tool suggests websites and other Display Network placements

Display Campaigns Tools

The Placement Tool

If you want to find specific placements on the GDN but you're not sure where to begin, try the Placement Tool shown in Figure 9-2, found under the "Tools and Analysis" tab. It looks similar to the Keyword Tool, but it returns a list of potential placements instead.

To use the tool, enter a word or phrase, a website or a select a category. You can refine the suggestions by location, language, device, and ad size, as well as user profile information like age, gender, household income, and education.

Clicking the Search button returns a list of placements that fit the specified criteria. Now, select Placements and add directly to the account from the tool. For large lists, you may wish to download the list.

Clicking a suggested placement displays high level information like where on the site ads can appear, content categories, the ad types and sizes available, a description, and a link to the Ad Planner Profile.

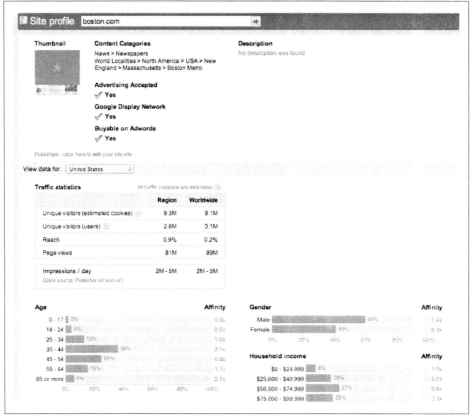

Figure 9-3. Ad Planner profile for Boston.com

DoubleClick Ad Planner

If advertising on the GDN is high priority, try Google's media planning too, the DoubleClick Ad Planner (*http://goo.gl/D1owx*). This free resource helps you build media plans to target websites visited by your target audience.

Use Ad Planner to accomplish the following tasks:

- Create audiences by demographics and interests.
- Find websites relevant to your audience. View site profiles (Figure 9-3) that help you make decisions about which placements to add.
- See aggregated statistics for millions of websites in more than 40 countries.
- Create lists of websites where you'd like to advertise and store them in a media plan.
- View aggregated website statistics for your media plan.

Want to learn more? Visit the Ad Planner Help Center at *http://goo.gl/tWs9m.*

Contextual Targeting Tool

The Contextual Targeting Tool, found under the "Tools and Analysis" tab, Figure 9-4 is a relatively new tool designed to automatically create ad groups and keyword lists for campaigns on the Google Display Network.

To use it, type up to 10 words or phrases separated by commas. Specify location and language to refine results.

The tool returns a list of suggested ad groups with 5-20 keyword suggestions for that ad group, plus a suggested bid. Clicking the   button displays more related groups of keywords. The   button leads to a list of predicted placements on the Display Network.

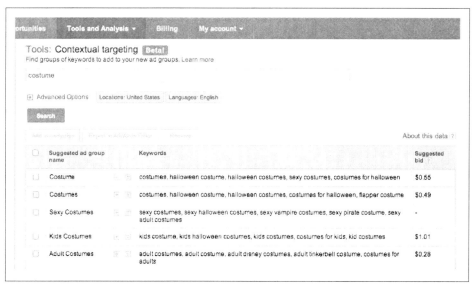

Figure 9-4. The Contextual Targeting Tool suggests new ad groups and keyword lists

Top 10 GDN Tips

Here are 10 tips for using the Google Display Network effectively.

1. *If you're brand new to AdWords, save the Display Network for later.* AdWords turns the GDN on by default for new campaigns. If this is your first time using AdWords, turn this network off in the campaign settings (in the networks section). Once you are comfortable using AdWords and interpreting the results, try the GDN to see if you can make it work for your advertising goals.

2. *Create separate campaigns for the GDN.* Your advertising strategy for the GDN is very different than the strategy for search. Keyword lists will be shorter, to help AdWords determine an appropriate theme. Ad creative may be different. Bids may be lower, or you may choose CPM bidding. I prefer to separate GDN campaigns

so all these differences can be managed and monitored. It's also helpful because I can assign a specific budget to the GDN, which cannot cannibalize search campaigns.

3. *Make image and video ads stand out.* Use bright, colorful ads that instantly communicate the intent of the ad (or are so enticing that the visitor simply has to click to learn more). Do not count on a visitor watching a video ad for any extended period of time. Communicate the most important messages early on. For specific placements, consider creating ads that complement the design and palette of the website. Your hot pink ad might work well on some websites; on others, the colors might clash and turn off prospects.

4. *Try CPM bidding.* CPM bidding can increase opportunities for image and video ads with a placement targeted campaign. CPM bidding ensures that Google is paid when ads are delivered, whether someone clicks or not, so CPM may help increase exposure for image and video ads on competitive sites.

5. *Filter unwanted placements using exclusions.* At the bottom of the Display Network roll-up tab under Placements, you see a link to Exclusions. This allows you to exclude particular websites or pages within a website at the ad group and campaign level by keyword, placements, topics, audiences, and categories.

6. *Use negative keywords.* Just as you would in a search campaign, include negative keywords to help AdWords prevent ads from showing on irrelevant web pages.

7. *Use campaign settings.* Most campaign settings applicable to search can refine GDN campaigns. For example, apply geotargeting so only visitors from your target area are eligible to see your ads.

8. *Ad all creative variations.* If AdWords identifies an ideal placement for your campaign but you don't have the right creative, you're out of luck. For example, AdWords might identify the perfect website to display your ads, but the site only accepts 728 × 90 image ads. If your creative includes 468 × 60 image ads only, you lose the advertising opportunity because your creative did not fit the website. Check out the Display Ad Builder in the Ads roll-up tab, which allows you to export ads in multiple sizes.

9. *Allot time for approvals.* Image and video ads must be manually reviewed and approved by Google, to ensure content is "family-safe." If you're planning a time-sensitive campaign, upload the ad as soon as it's ready, with a Paused status. AdWords now reviews paused ads. With any luck, your ad will be pre-approved to go live on the appointed date.

10. *Always be testing.* As with anything in AdWords, you should constantly test campaigns to make improvements. For GDN campaigns, try different colors and layouts for ads, different ad text variations, and different placements and topics. Experiment with different calls to action and conversion incentives to improve conversion rate.

CHAPTER 10

Additional Ad Formats

The Google Display Network offers many additional places for ads to appear and ad formats like image, Flash, and video. This chapter covers additional ad formats, including technical specifications, editorial guidelines, and tips for success.

Image and Flash Ads

AdWords accepts *.gif*, *.jpg*, *.png*, and *.swf* files in the following dimensions (measured in pixels):

- 300 × 50 (mobile leaderboard)
- 468 × 60 (banner)
- 728 × 90 (leaderboard)
- 250 × 250 (square)
- 200 × 200 (small square)
- 336 × 280 (large rectangle)
- 300 × 250 (inline rectangle)
- 120 × 600 (skyscraper)
- 160 × 600 (wide skyscraper)

Let's review the technical and editorial rules for image and Flash ads. First, the file size is limited to 50 KB. The accepted dimensions vary site-to-site, depending on the website publisher. For example, if a website accepts 728 × 90 ads, it's up to the advertiser to provide an appropriately-sized leaderboard ad. AdWords does not resize images. Each ad is accompanied by a display URL and a destination URL; the rules for text ad URLs apply to these formats, too.

AdWords is specific about what advertiser can and cannot do with image and Flash ads. The point of the rules is to make it clear that an ad is indeed an ad. (Example rules: the ad cannot mimic a dialog box or system warning, it must fill the ad space completely, and it cannot "segment" to appear like multiple ads.) All ads fall into one of three categories: Family Safe, Non-Family Safe, and Adult Sexual Content; image and video ads must be Family Safe to be approved. Visit the AdWords Policy Center (*http://goo .gl/zDRB3*) to see the most recent requirements.

Flash ads are subject to the same rules as image ads, with additional technical rules. Ads must be published for Flash Player version 4–10; ActionScript versions 1–3 are accepted. AdWords uses the `clickTAG` variable to track Flash ads, so this must be included exactly as AdWords specifies. For more information and parameter code examples, see the Additional Requirements for Flash Ads (*http://goo.gl/Mm3bR*) section in the Policy Center. AdWords checks code when Flash ads are uploaded; if they do not adhere to all rules, the ads won't be accepted and you see an error message like "Encountered Flash error—ad cannot have a URL."

To create an image or Flash ad, visit the Ads roll-up tab in an ad group and click "+New ad," as shown in Figure 10-1.

Figure 10-1. Create image or Flash ads

Now, upload the file from your computer (see Figure 10-2), give it a name to identify it in the account, a display URL and a destination URL. Click "Save ad."

The new ad is listed as "Under review" (see Figure 10-3) until someone at AdWords reviews the creative to make sure it complies with the editorial guidelines. If the ad is disapproved, upload a different file for reconsideration. Occasionally a perfectly acceptable image is disapproved because of human error during the review process. If you are sure the ad complies with all rules, resubmit and it may be approved on the second round.

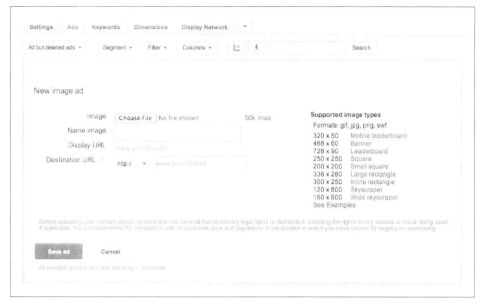

Figure 10-2. Upload the image

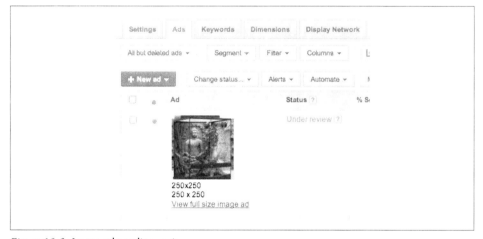

Figure 10-3. Image ad pending review

The Display Ad Builder

Need help creating a display ad? AdWords offers a web-based tool for creating image and Flash ads. It's found in the Ads roll-up tab, under the "+New ad" drop-down.

The Display Ad Builder offers a gallery of templates organized by theme like seasons, events, and industries. You can customize colors, fonts, text, images, and URLs to create your own ad based on a selected template.

Start by selecting a template for your ad. Then you can customize it, as shown in Figure 10-4. Give the ad a name, customize the verbiage, upload product images and logos (optional), change colors and fonts, and specify a display and destination URL.

Once you enter the information, a preview of the ad appears. Clicking the icons shows how the ad renders in various sizes. To see all versions of the ad in one place, click the link "Select ad sizes." Now you see a preview with every variation, shown in Figure 10-5. Select and deselect ads as you wish.

Video Ads

AdWords offers several video ad formats, including "click-to-play," in-stream video, in-video static image ads, TrueView videos, and others. To create a video ads, select the "Display Ad Builder" option from the "+New ad" drop-down in the Ads roll-up tab.

Click-to-play videos are initiated by the website visitor. People who see the ad must click to view a video. If the viewer clicks a second time or on the Display URL, she is taken to the ad's destination URL. Pricing depends on the model selected by the advertiser, CPC or CPM. With CPC, you do not pay when someone plays the video; the charge occurs when the viewer clicks through to the destination URL.

With CPC bidding, clickthrough rate is an important factor in the auction, so ads with low CTR may have a difficult time winning placements. With CPM bidding, you pay for every 1,000 impressions the ad's opening image receives. With this pricing model, CTR is not as important because clicks are not part of the equation.

Another pricing model available is called cost-per-view (CPV). This options is available for TrueView video ads. With TrueView ads, you pay when a viewer deliberately plays your video or chooses to continue watching when it loads as they browse video content. Unlike CPC and CPM, you do not to pay every time an ad is shown. TrueView ads appear on YouTube and other GDN sites for desktop computers and high-end mobile devices.

To create a video ad, select the Display Ad Builder option from the "New ad" drop-down menu. (See Figure 10-6.) Click the Video category, under the "Media and Channels" section. Then, select the template for the video ad you want to create. For click-to-play, you need an opening image and a video file. You can add an optional closing image. The image ad file size is limited to 50 KB, with two dimensions options: 336 × 280 or 300 × 250. The video file must be 75 MB or less, with a runtime of four minutes or less.

AdWords accepts the following video file formats: ASF, AVI, MP4, MPEG, Quicktime, and Windows Media. Visit the AdWords Policy Center to see the complete technical requirements: *http://goo.gl/FVIWJ*.

In-stream video ads places a 15- or 30-second video ad within video content on websites. Some placements run a 300 × 60 or 300 × 250 companion banner with the video

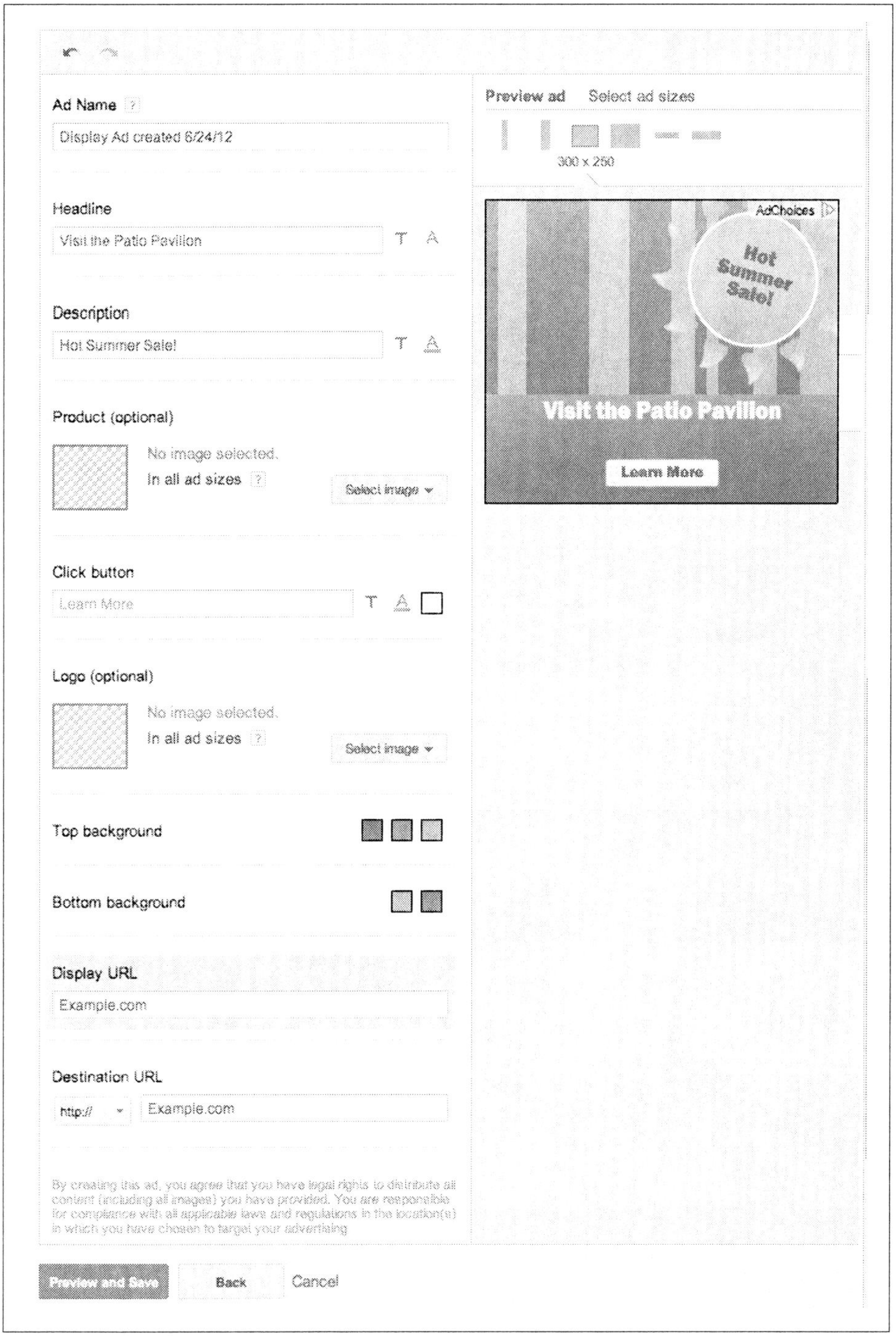

Figure 10-4. Create professional ads with the Display Ad Builder

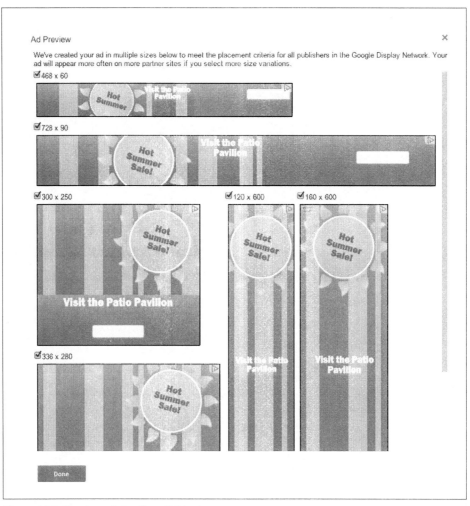

Figure 10-5. Preview ads in all available sizes

ad. An in-video image ad places a 480 × 70 image over video content on websites. Some sites run a 300 × 250 companion banner. Visit the AdWords Policy Center (*http://goo .gl/hKYJt*) to see the complete technical requirements for these formats.

Mobile Ads

AdWords offers text and image ads for mobile devices. People who see the ads are sent to a mobile web page or click to initiate a phone call. The requirements for running these ads vary depending on whether the device has a full Internet browser or it's a WAP device. For full browsers, the requirements are identical to text ads on desktop

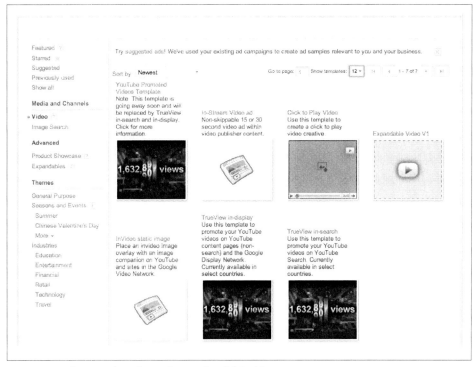

Figure 10-6. Create video ads via the Display Ad Builder

and laptop computers, except that the landing page cannot use Flash. Flash image ads are not allowed for any mobile devices.

WAP mobile text ads appear on Google's Search and Display Network; mobile image ads appear on the mobile Display Network only. With WAP ads, there are differences for both text and image ads. Text ads are three lines. Headlines are limited to 18 characters (12 characters for Japanese, 9 characters for Chinese), 18 characters for the description line (12 characters for Japanese, 9 for Chinese), and 20 characters for the display URL. WAP image ad options vary depending on the device's aspect ratio.

For 6:1 aspect ratio, available formats include 300 × 50 (7.5 KB max), 216 × 36 (4.5 KB max), and 168 × 28 (3 KB max). For devices with 4:1 aspect ratio, available formats include 300 × 75 (7.5 KB max), 216 × 54 (4.5 KB max), and 168 × 42 (3 KB max).

WAP ads require a mobile-compliant landing page. AdWords supports WML (WAP 1.x), XHTML (WAP 2.0), CHTML (imode, etc.), and PDA-compliant HTML.

If you plan to run mobile ads, it's a good idea to set them up in a separate campaign targeting only mobile devices (see Figure 10-7). There will be differences in the keywords selected and the bids you choose. Keywords on mobile phones may be shorter than those you choose for campaigns targeting desktops and laptops; after all, the keyboard is much smaller, so the queries are often shorter. If you separate the campaigns you can write ads specifically targeting mobile devices (e.g., "Call Us Now!").

Figure 10-7. Select mobile devices only

To create a WAP ad, visit the Ads roll-up tab in an ad group and click "+New ad," as shown in Figure 10-8.

Figure 10-8. Create a WAP mobile ad

Now, select the type of WAP ad you want to create, text or image. With the text version, you can link to a mobile web page or initiate a phone call. (See Figure 10-9.)

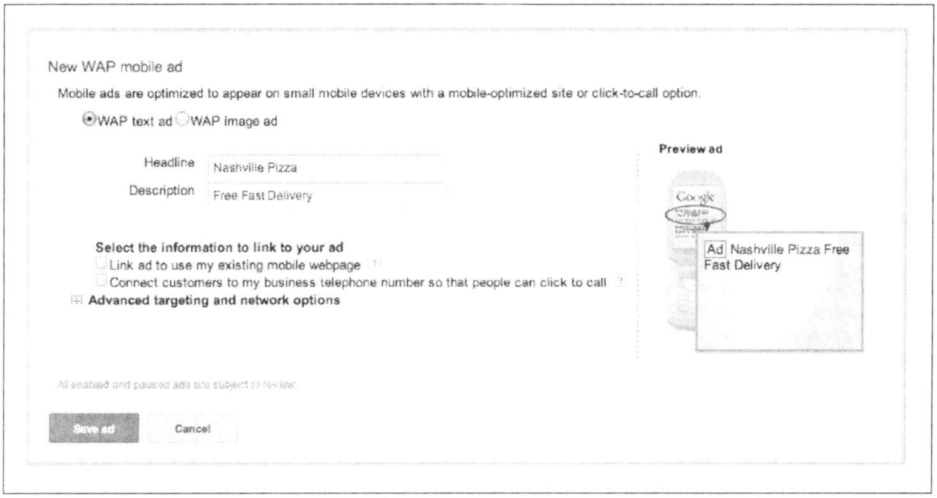

Figure 10-9. Create a WAP text ad

And that's it! A few additional rules for WAP click-to-call ads: calls must connect customers to the business, and the number must be local or domestic to the targeted country. International calls must include the national direct dialing (NDD) prefix, but not the country code. AdWords does not allow telephone numbers that require additional payment by the caller, fax numbers, or emergency phone numbers.

Image and Video Tips

Here are some tips for creating effective image and video ads.

1. *Make pretty ads.* Attractive ads are more likely to catch a prospect's attention. Try to enticing them with high-quality images. If you're targeting specific placements, consider creating ads that complement the design and palette of the website.

2. *Create various ad sizes.* If you show ads on the Display Network using automatic placements, AdWords identifies sites on your behalf. The system might find the perfect spot for an ad, that accepts a 468 x 60 image ad. If you did not include that size image in your ad group, you miss the opportunity to show an ad.

3. *Experiment.* Like text ads, experiment with variations of image and video ads to see which return greater results. Experiment with colors, templates, calls to action, and content to see what works best.

4. *Don't assume people will watch the video.* When creating a video, it's best to assume that users won't watch it. In this case, only the opening image will be seen. It's a good idea to treat it as a standalone image ad. Make sure it has your branding, a call to action and compelling, attractive photos. Google's studies have shown that non-commercial opening images often have greater playrate.

5. *If they do watch the video, make it short and sweet.* Web users are an impatient bunch. Unless you've got a hit video, like the Old Spice Guy, chances are they won't watch the entire video. Keep your marketing message short, clear and front loaded. Videos can be four minutes long, but it's best to shoot for 30 seconds or less.

6. *Track performance.* Once live, monitor how ads perform using campaign statistics on the Ads and Dimensions roll-up tabs. You can view reports on free click interactions to see if people use special interactive ad formats.

7. *Don't be a hack.* If you are not a graphic designer, it's probably best to hire someone to make your ads. Many freelancers and agencies specialize in graphic design for online campaigns. The Display Ad Builder is the next best option. If you decide to use it, take the time to write good copy and find high quality images to customize it (it's easy to make an ugly ad).

CHAPTER 11

Bids, Budgets, and Billing, Oh My

How Bidding Works

Cost-per-click bidding (CPC) is also referred to as pay-per-click (PPC). It's a pricing model where an advertiser pays only for clicks on ads. An ad can display one million times, but if no one clicks, it does not cost the advertiser. Naturally it's in Google's best interests to show ads that receive clicks; keywords with higher clickthrough rate (CTR) are rewarded with better Quality Scores.

There are several bidding models available. This chapter explains how each model works, how AdWords calculates actual costs, and what billing options are available to advertisers.

Manual Maximum CPC bidding

The default bidding option is *manual maximum CPC bidding*, shown in Figure 11-1. This model specifies the maximum amount you are willing to pay for an ad click. Bids are set at the ad group level and the keyword level.

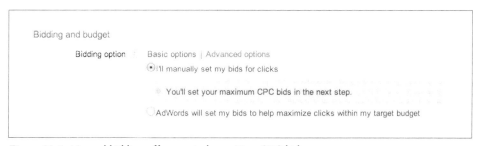

Figure 11-1. Manual bidding offers control over Max CPC bids

Bidding and budget

Bidding option ?   Basic options | Advanced options

⦿ Focus on **clicks** - use maximum CPC bids

○ I'll manually set my bids for clicks

⦿ AdWords will set my bids to help maximize clicks within my target budget

☑ CPC bid limit ? $ 2

Figure 11-2. With automatic bidding, it's a good idea to specify a CPC bid limit

Automatic Bidding

Automatic bidding allows AdWords to manage your bids. This model tries to generate the most clicks possible within the budget. By default, the system automatically chooses whatever bids it determines will earn the most clicks.

The automatic bidding model finds clicks, nothing more. It does not help achieve higher conversions, profitable ad positions, or lower click costs. If you use this model, I recommend specifying a bid limit. To access, click the "Advanced options" link to see the checkbox labeled "CPC bid limit." Enter an amount, as shown in Figure 11-2. Otherwise, you may pay far more for a click than makes sense for your business. The bid limit applies to all ad groups in the campaign, and prevents AdWords from showing ads in extremely competitive, expensive auctions.

If you are brand-new and have no idea what price range to bid on keywords, using automatic bidding for a short period of time can help you learn what clicks cost. You can then switch to manual bidding with that data.

Enhanced CPC Bidding

One easy way to improve conversion performance is to enable *enhanced CPC bidding*, shown in Figure 11-3.

To use it, you must have conversion tracking set up in the account (see Chapter 12). The feature does not require a minimum number of conversions, so you can turn it on immediately. If the campaign does not have any recorded conversions, enhanced CPC has no effect on the bids. But, once conversions start recording, enhanced CPC can use the data to raise or lower bids if a conversion is more or less likely.

Enhanced CPC can raise a bid as much as 30 percent if a conversion is likely. If AdWords data shows a conversion is less likely, it can reduce the bid with no bottom limit. The daily budget still applies, so overall costs do not increase.

Figure 11-3. Enhanced CPC uses conversion tracking data to dynamically adjust bids

Figure 11-4. With CPM bidding, specify a maximum bid for every 1,000 ad impressions

CPM Bidding

Unlike CPC bidding, *CPM bidding* works on a pay-per-impression model. Specify a maximum price you are willing to pay for every 1,000 times an ad is displayed, whether it is clicked on or not. An ad click does not incur an additional cost.

CPM bidding is available for the Google Display Network only. If Search is selected in the campaign settings, the CPM option does not appear as a bidding option. Figure 11-4 shows CPM bidding, labeled "Focus on impressions—use maximum CPM bids."

Base your CPM bid on the value of ad exposure to your business. Experiment with bids to see what price ranges work for your campaigns. CPM bids vary depending on the targeted sites. If the managed placements include extremely competitive websites like *www.nytimes.com*, bid aggressively to win placement in the auctions. If you don't want placements on competitive sites, set lower bids.

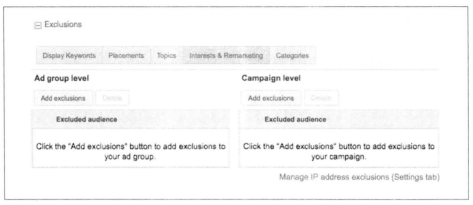

Figure 11-5. Exclude by category

The Placements section in the Display Network roll-up tab shows which websites, and which pages on those sites, displayed your ads. Based on this data, focus on or exclude particular placements.

CPM bidding works well if you want to show image and video ads. These formats are often more competitive and expensive, particularly with CPC bidding.

There is a handy feature available in the Display Network roll-up tab that can helps target ads to appropriate web pages and potentially improve the effectiveness of CPM campaigns. Click the Exclusions link at the bottom of the page, then select Categories, as shown in Figure 11-5.

Now, a window appears showing filters available for ads on the Google Display Network. You can prevent ads from appearing on pages with specific types of content, like "death and tragedy," "profanity," or "sexually suggestive content." You can exclude formats like in-game ads, and page types like parked domains and error pages.

For CPM campaigns, you pay if an ad appears on the page, whether someone sees it or not. If the ad appears at the bottom of a long web page, the impression counts, whether someone scrolled to the bottom or not. To increase the likelihood that the ad is seen, try the "Below the fold" exclusion shown in Figure 11-6. This prevents ads from appearing on pages where people need to scroll down to see the ads.

AdWords considers an ad above the fold if it is 100 percent on-screen when the browser window loads. AdWords considers individual user settings and preferences like web browser, monitor size, and screen resolution to make this determination.

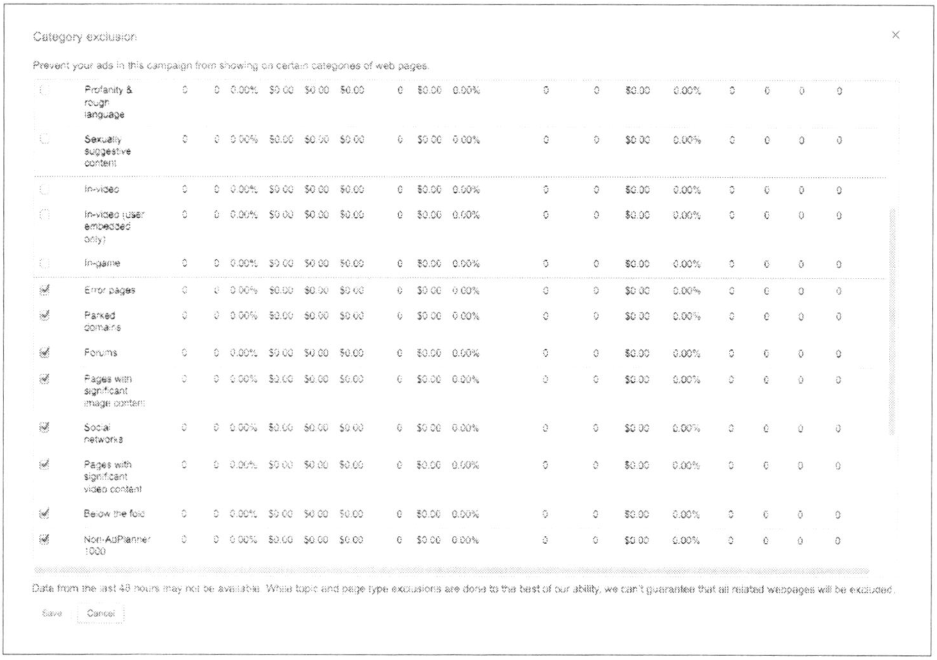

Category exclusion   ×

Prevent your ads in this campaign from showing on certain categories of web pages.

☐	Profanity & rough language	0	0	0.00%	$0.00	$0.00	$0.00	0	$0.00	0.00%	0	0	$0.00	0.00%	0	0
☐	Sexually suggestive content	0	0	0.00%	$0.00	$0.00	$0.00	0	$0.00	0.00%	0	0	$0.00	0.00%	0	0
☐	In-video	0	0	0.00%	$0.00	$0.00	$0.00	0	$0.00	0.00%	0	0	$0.00	0.00%	0	0
☐	In-video (user embedded only)	0	0	0.00%	$0.00	$0.00	$0.00	0	$0.00	0.00%	0	0	$0.00	0.00%	0	0
☐	In-game	0	0	0.00%	$0.00	$0.00	$0.00	0	$0.00	0.00%	0	0	$0.00	0.00%	0	0
☑	Error pages	0	0	0.00%	$0.00	$0.00	$0.00	0	$0.00	0.00%	0	0	$0.00	0.00%	0	0
☑	Parked domains	0	0	0.00%	$0.00	$0.00	$0.00	0	$0.00	0.00%	0	0	$0.00	0.00%	0	0
☑	Forums	0	0	0.00%	$0.00	$0.00	$0.00	0	$0.00	0.00%	0	0	$0.00	0.00%	0	0
☑	Pages with significant image content	0	0	0.00%	$0.00	$0.00	$0.00	0	$0.00	0.00%	0	0	$0.00	0.00%	0	0
☑	Social networks	0	0	0.00%	$0.00	$0.00	$0.00	0	$0.00	0.00%	0	0	$0.00	0.00%	0	0
☑	Pages with significant video content	0	0	0.00%	$0.00	$0.00	$0.00	0	$0.00	0.00%	0	0	$0.00	0.00%	0	0
☑	Below the fold	0	0	0.00%	$0.00	$0.00	$0.00	0	$0.00	0.00%	0	0	$0.00	0.00%	0	0
☑	Non-AdPlanner 1000	0	0	0.00%	$0.00	$0.00	$0.00	0	$0.00	0.00%	0	0	$0.00	0.00%	0	0

Data from the last 48 hours may not be available. While topic and page type exclusions are done to the best of our ability, we can't guarantee that all related webpages will be excluded.

Save   Cancel

Figure 11-6. Category exclusions prevent ads from appearing alongside particular categories of content, on particular types of web pages, or on particular areas of web pages on the Google Display Network

Conversion Optimizer

My favorite bidding model is Conversion Optimizer. It enables intelligent bidding, because it has access to multi-dimensional data you can't see with manual bidding. Many accounts experience double-digit increases in conversions and decreases in overall cost per acquisition with this bidding model.

So how does Conversion Optimizer work?

Unlike other bidding models, Conversion Optimizer works toward a *cost-per-acquisition* (CPA) goal. Rather than give AdWords a maximum bid, advertisers provide a maximum or target CPA. Max CPA represents the most you are willing to pay for a conversion. Target CPA represents the average amount you are willing to pay for a conversion.

You still pay per click, but Conversion Optimizer manages bids in real time. Using historical information about the campaign, Conversion Optimizer dynamically generates a unique CPC bid for each auction. This bid reflects the predicted likelihood of a conversion, based on conversion history, the keyword's broad match query, the searcher's geographic location, browser and language, time of day, and historical conversion rates on Google Search, the Search Partners and the Display Network.

Actual CPA depends on factors outside of AdWords, since conversion rate is affected by ad changes, website changes, and increased advertiser competition. If the actual conversion rate is lower than the predicted conversion rate, actual CPA may exceed the bid.

Incidentally, the Display Network is not required to use Conversion Optimizer. The only requirement is that conversion tracking be enabled, with a 15 conversion minimum in the last 30 days in that campaign. AdWords recommends running conversion tracking for a two-week minimum before enabling Conversion Optimizer.

In general, the bidding option works best for campaigns with higher numbers of conversions with a relatively steady conversion rate. If the keywords have significant seasonal fluctuations, Conversion Optimizer may not be able to make appropriate conversion predictions when traffic changes.

Conversion Optimizer tips

1. Be sure to track meaningful conversions. Visits to the landing page are not conversions.

2. Give it some time. Conversion Optimizer needs to "learn" what works and what doesn't work. When you turn it on, there may be an adjustment period where costs increase and conversions decrease. I recommend at least a day or two to adjust.

3. As long as you maintain 15 conversions in a single campaign in the last 30 days, you can switch back and forth between manual bidding and Conversion Optimizer. It's best to use Conversion Optimizer for campaigns that have been tracking conversions for at least 14 days.

4. More is more. The more conversion data you have, the better Conversion Optimizer's predictions can be.

5. Experiment with the CPA bids to learn where profits are maximized.

6. Be careful making changes to conversion tracking and significant campaign changes while using Conversion Optimizer.

Figure 11-7 shows Conversion Optimizer, labeled "Focus on conversions (Conversion Optimizer)."

AdWords Discounter and Smart Pricing

AdWords includes two automatic pricing discount features, the AdWords Discounter and smart pricing. You cannot turn these features on or off, but their effect is seen in the actual costs per click.

The AdWords Discounter is applied automatically. You may notice that in many cases actual cost-per-click is lower than the maximum cost-per-click. After ads are ranked, AdWords Discounter adjusts actual CPCs so you pay the minimum amount required

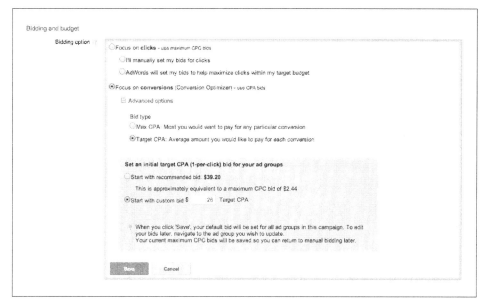

Figure 11-7. Conversion Optimizer is available for campaigns with 15+ recorded conversions in the last 30 days

to exceed the ad rank of the next advertiser. This does not mean the actual cost-per-click will always be lower than the Max CPC bid, but it is often the case.

Smart pricing automatically reduces the actual cost per click if a click from the Google Display Network is less likely to result in a conversion. The likelihood of the conversion is based on AdWords' historical conversion data for the types of keywords in the ad group and the type of website on the Display Network.

How to Decide What to Bid

If you are not sure how much to bid on a keyword or how much you can spend per day on the selected keywords, use the Traffic Estimator tool found in the "Tools and Analysis" tab.

The Traffic Estimator provides a (very ballpark) idea how a keyword will perform in the account. You can set specific targeting criteria, including geotargets, language and networks. Then, manually add keywords to test or upload a file of keywords to see a report. You can upload .csv files created with Excel, the Keyword Tool and AdWords Editor.

To use the tool, enter the proposed keyword or a set of keywords, a Max CPC, and a daily budget, as shown in Figure 11-8. The tool shows you, keyword by keyword, an estimate of the clicks, impressions, ad position, cost, CTR and CPC you might expect each day.

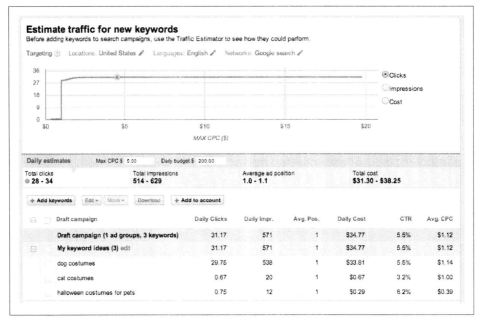

Figure 11-8. The Traffic Estimator shows how new keywords can impact the account

The Bid Simulator

AdWords does not tell you the minimum bid required for a top-ranked ad, but there is one feature that can help make an estimate. Called the bid simulator, it appears in the Max CPC column for keywords. You see it displayed as a small icon below the bid; click the symbol to access it ($^{\$0.92}$). Once you click the symbol, a window opens, as shown in Figure 11-9.

The feature is not always available. If the campaign reached or nearly reached the daily budget at least once in the past week, it does not display. So how does it work? The bid simulator recalculates all AdWords auctions on Google and the Search Network from the past seven days for that keyword. Using internal auction data like Quality Score, the simulator displays estimates the impressions an ad might have received with different (usually higher) Max CPC bids.

The estimates are separated by all impressions and top impressions. "Top impressions" refers to top-ranked ads that appear in the shaded box above the search results, and applies to Google Search only. The estimator does not consider performance on the Google Display Network. You can change bids from the simulator interface.

One important note: the bid simulator reports on the last seven days, but it cannot predict future performance. If the next week is expected to be different from the pre-

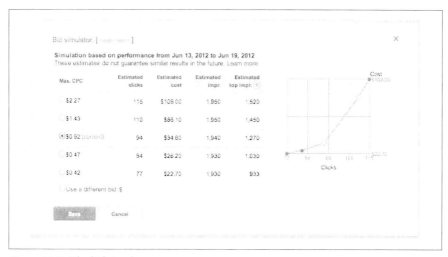

Figure 11-9. The bid simulator

vious week, in regards to traffic and competition, you may want to adjust bids accordingly.

Understanding Billing Options

Billing options vary depending on the advertiser's country and currency. In the United States there are default billing options, *postpay* and *prepay*. These options may be labeled "Automatic payments" and "Manual payments."

Use this form to see which payment options are available for your country/currency: *http://goo.gl/dIuoM*.

For postpay or automatic payments, you pay Google after ads run. You are charged when you reach the credit limit (called the "billing threshold"), or in 30 days, whichever comes first. You can use a credit card, a debit card, or directly debit from a bank account. If it's critical that ads run at all times without interruption, it's a good idea to add a backup credit card. This prevents potential downtime if AdWords cannot charge the primary card.

For prepay or manual payments, you pay in advance before ads run. Payment options include credit card, debit card and bank transfer.

I prefer postpay. With prepay accounts, the interface constantly delivers warnings that the prepaid balance is low. If you forget to add funds when the balance is depleted, ads stop appearing. On the other hand, if you use prepay it's a reminder how much you pay to advertise, which may encourage you to scrutinize performance more carefully. You can switch pricing models any time.

Applying Promotional Credits

Google occasionally distributes AdWords advertising credits. Credits are usually restricted to new accounts, defined as having been created within the last 14 days. An account older than 14 days is not considered new, even if billing details were not provided or if ads never ran. Some promotional codes are applicable to existing accounts—when in doubt, try to apply it.

To apply an advertising credit to a new account, complete the following steps:

1. Login to AdWords.
2. Click the Billing tab and select "Billing preferences" from the drop-down menu. From here, enter billing information.
3. Select the country or territory where the billing address is located.
4. Entire billing details (name, address, phone number).
5. Next, specify how ads will be paid for, postpay or prepay.
6. Now, enter billing information, either a credit or debit card or bank information for direct debit.
7. On this page, look for the line item that reads: "Do you have a promotional code?" Click the link and enter the promotional code.
8. Agree to Google's terms and conditions and you're good to go!

To apply a credit to an existing AdWords account, the steps are different.

1. Login to AdWords.
2. Click the Billing tab and select the Billing Preferences page.
3. At the bottom, look for the "Promotional Codes" section. Enter your code, select "Google AdWords " from the account drop-down menu and click Redeem.

Troubleshooting promotional codes

Many people have trouble applying promotional codes. Here are some troubleshooting tips.

- If you received the code electronically, copy and paste the code rather than manually typing it. Do not include extra spaces before or after the code.
- If you received the code via print material, be sure not to type the letter O for a zero, or vice versa. If your code doesn't work, try switching these characters to see if that corrects the problem.
- You cannot apply a promotional code to an account before providing payment information (a credit card, a debit card, or bank account information).

- If your account is on monthly invoicing terms, you cannot apply advertising credits to your account. Your Google client representative can apply credits to your account on your behalf.
- If your account is set up through the Google Grants (*http://goo.gl/DHWcO*) program, you cannot apply an advertising credit (your advertising is already free). To take advantage of a promotional credit, consider opening a second, standard AdWords account. Use this account to advertise on the Google Display Network, an option excluded from Google Grants accounts. Google Grants caps bids at $1; use the standard account for keywords that require higher bids to compete effectively in the AdWords auction.
- You cannot apply promotional codes when logged into a manager account (called My Client Center (*http://goo.gl/pCB9z*)). You must log in with the managed account's username and password. If you manage accounts for clients and do not have their passwords, ask your client to apply the promotional code or request temporary access as a user with Standard or Administrative access.

Monthly Invoicing

Some advertisers with large monthly advertising budgets prefer monthly invoices rather than prepay or postpay billing. With monthly invoicing, sometimes referred to as *credit terms* or *invoicing terms*, Google extends a line of credit for serving ads and sends an invoice each month. Payment for ad delivery is by check or wire transfer.

You must apply and be approved for monthly invoicing.

A handy perk: unlike standard AdWords account, where the daily budget is the sum of all campaign budgets, invoicing accounts can use account-level budgets. Account budgets do not replace campaign budgets; they simply serve as a spending cap. With monthly invoicing you can specify when ads start and stop, control costs accrued in a set time period, and assign a PO number for invoices.

To apply for monthly invoicing, contact AdWords via their contact form (*http://goo.gl/nXv1S*) or talk to your AdWords account representative.

Click Fraud

Click fraud, discreetly referred to as "invalid clicks" or "invalid activity" in the AdWords Help Center, is a reality of online advertising. Occasional fraudulent clicks are the cost of doing business online. If your unhappy ex decides to click once on your ad, AdWords may not be able to recognize that the click stemmed from petty retribution. If your ex is *really* unhappy with you and clicks on the ad multiple times, AdWords recognizes invalid behavior and removes that activity and associated costs from your account.

Google takes click fraud very seriously because the success of the AdWords business model depends on happy advertisers. If advertisers believe budgets are wasted on competitors and enemies, they will be understandably reluctant to continue advertising.

To combat click fraud, AdWords analyzes each click, considering various data points like IP address, the time of the click, duplicate clicks, and click patterns. AdWords uses this data to try to filter fraudulent clicks before they appear in account reports. To protect advertisers, AdWords discards suspicious activity, like repetitive clicks, as well as clicks and impressions from known sources of "invalid activity."

 If you see suspicious activity in AdWords, follow up with AdWords to find out what is going on. Start at the Invalid Clicks Troubleshooter: *http://goo.gl/vct6k*.

CHAPTER 12

Measuring Success

What Are Your Goals?

Before spending a dime on Google AdWords, ask yourself this question—why am I doing this?

It seems obvious, but many new advertisers mistakenly consider the appearance of an ad, or an ad click, a measure of success. You pay Google for leads, typically measured by clicks on ads. From Google's perspective, an ad click is indeed success—AdWords delivered the lead, and Google made money. As shown in Figure 12-1, Groupon is willing to pay a specified amount if a person clicks on its top-ranked ad. But, the click is not Groupon's ultimate goal.

The real objective is what happens *after* the click. You pay Google for ad clicks, so it makes sense to want something tangible in return. The broad goals may be obvious—grow the business, drive traffic to a website, acquire members, etc. With AdWords, you can track if an ad click results in a desirable behavior, called a *conversion*. In Groupon's case, a conversion might be counted when someone registers, as in Figure 12-2.

Figure 12-1. Groupon uses AdWords to connect potential customers with their daily deal

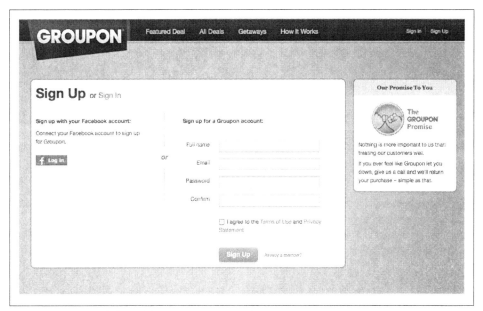

Figure 12-2. Track if clicks deliver conversions, such as a registration

Start by defining your goals. Do you want to increase registrations by a certain percentage? Do you want to sell 100 products each week? Your goal might be to receive five phone inquiries each day from AdWords or display an ad 1,000 times for a certain price on a specific website. You can track multiple conversions in the same AdWords account.

In the Groupon example, AdWords can track if an ad click resulted in a registration, as well as a purchase, shown in Figure 12-3.

Whatever the desired outcome, hold AdWords accountable and make changes to optimize performance.

Figure 12-3. This example has multiple conversions: a registration and a sale

Once you know what you want, the next step is to track it and measure it. Let's review some options to track performance.

Conversion Tracking

One of the simplest ways to track success is a feature called *Conversion Tracking*. Conversion Tracking shows whether an ad click resulted in a desirable behavior on the website. It places a cookie on the searcher's computer after a click on an ad. This cookie expires in 30 days.

If at any point during that 30-day period a conversion page is reached on that computer, it is recorded in AdWords. The conversion is credited to the keyword that triggered the ad, on the date of the click. Conversions do not appear in the AdWords account immediately; there is a full 24-hour reporting delay.

There are two types of conversions shown in the account.

1-per-click conversions count a conversion for every ad click resulting in a conversion. If multiple conversion happens after a single ad click, like the Groupon example above,

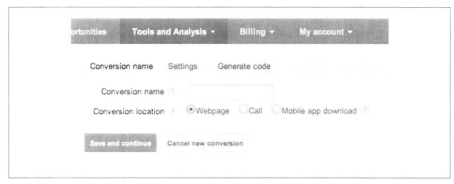

Figure 12-4. Give the conversion a name and location

only the first conversion counts. Use this to measure conversions indicating unique customer acquisitions (such as signing up for Groupon's email).

Many-per-click conversions also count a conversions, but includes multiple conversions that result from the same click. Groupon would see that two conversions resulted from the above example: a sign up and a purchase.

Setup is simple. Select Conversions from the "Tools and Analysis" drop-down menu. Create a conversion by clicking the "+New conversion" button. The wizard walks you through the setup.

1. Give the conversion a name to identify it in the account, as shown in Figure 12-4. Select the conversion location—the place where customers will complete the conversion. There are three options: webpage, call, or mobile app download. Webpage tracks conversions on website pages, call tracks conversions with a trackable phone number, and mobile app download tracks conversions by downloads of mobile Android apps.

2. Specify a category (purchase/sale, signup, lead, view of a key page, or other).

3. Specify a page security level: *http* or *https*. Not sure? Use *http*.

4. Specify the markup language of the conversion page (HTML, CHTML, XHTML, or WML). If you're targeting a web page, in most cases, HTML works. The other options are specific to mobile devices. Chtml is used for mobile sites created using chtml; xhtml is used for sites targeting mobile browsers; wml used for mobile sites created using wml.

5. Specify the conversion value (optional). This field sets a monetary value for the conversion. The value cannot include a currency symbol and must have the decimal separator that corresponds to the interface language. For example, if the value for the conversion is $19.99 and the interface language is English, the correct value for the field is 19.99.

   If you have an ecommerce website, you can use dynamic variables, like the total value of the purchase. Inserting a dynamic value is usually done with a server side variable. Talk to your webmaster about setting this up—you need the variable name for your shopping cart's system.

6. Google encourages advertisers to inform website visitors if their actions are being tracked on a website. My preferred way to do that is to create a privacy policy/ terms of use page that discloses this information. If your website does not include a privacy policy, use the optional "Tracking indicator." When a conversion is completed, visitors sees a Google Site Stats box informing them that their actions were tracked. You can select a one- or two-line format, background color and language.

7. Advanced options→"View-through conversion window" sets a time frame for tracking *view-through-conversions*. A view-through conversion occurs when a person views an image or rich media ad on the Google Display Network and did not click, but later converts. The default window is 30 days; change that to whatever time frame you want.

8. Advanced options→"View-through conversion search de-duplication" determines how conversions are counted for people who saw an image or rich media ad on the Google Display Network *and* clicked on a text ad from Google Search. The default is disabled, which counts conversions as both view-through and clickthrough conversions. When enabled, conversions are counted only as clickthrough conversions. These steps are all shown in Figure 12-5.

9. Click "Save and continue."

10. Now, select who makes changes to the website. As shown in Figure 12-6, the options are "Someone else makes changes to the code" and "I make changes to the code."

 "Someone else" sends an email to an address you specify with the code and implementation instructions. Some email clients change line breaks in the JavaScript snippet and break it. To avoid this problem, copy the code, save it as a plain text document, and email as an attachment.

11. Click "Done" and conversion tracking is ready to go!

Once the code is placed on the conversion success page, tracking begins. Remember, the code is placed on the page that indicated success occurred, like a "thank you for your purchase" confirmation page. One common error is to put the code on an AdWords landing page, which results in 100 percent conversion rate (wouldn't that be nice?).

You see a list of the conversions under the Conversions tab. New conversions are labeled "Unverified" until a conversion happens. There is delay with conversion tracking reporting, so you will not see results for 24 hours after a conversion occurs.

Figure 12-5. Specify Conversion Tracking settings

Once a conversion occurs, you see conversion stats throughout the account, down to the keyword level. If you do not see conversion stats, customize the columns to enable them.

Search Funnels

Search Funnels enhance basic conversion reporting by providing eight additional reports. These reports show user behavior on Google.com (clicks and impressions) leading up to recorded conversions.

How is it different? Conversions in AdWords are attributed to the last ad clicked before the conversion. With Search Funnels, you see how keywords assist conversions before that last click. The conversions reported in Funnels reports are tracked by the AdWords Conversion Tracking or imported from Google Analytics. See Figure 12-7.

The reports include:

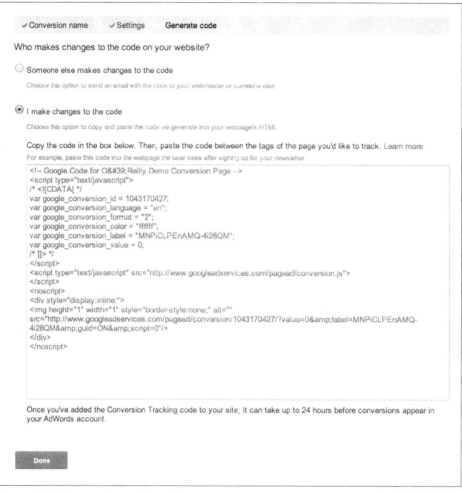

```
✓ Conversion name    ✓ Settings    Generate code

Who makes changes to the code on your website?

○ Someone else makes changes to the code
   Choose this option to send an email with the code to your webmaster or someone else

◉ I make changes to the code
   Choose this option to copy and paste the code we generate into your webpage's HTML

   Copy the code in the box below. Then, paste the code between the tags of the page you'd like to track. Learn more
   For example, paste this code into the webpage the user sees after signing up for your newsletter

   <!-- Google Code for O&#39;Reilly Demo Conversion Page -->
   <script type="text/javascript">
   /* <![CDATA[ */
   var google_conversion_id = 1043170427;
   var google_conversion_language = "en";
   var google_conversion_format = "2";
   var google_conversion_color = "ffffff";
   var google_conversion_label = "MNPiCLPEnAMQ-4i28QM";
   var google_conversion_value = 0;
   /* ]]> */
   </script>
   <script type="text/javascript" src="http://www.googleadservices.com/pagead/conversion.js">
   </script>
   <noscript>
   <div style="display:inline;">
   <img height="1" width="1" style="border-style:none;" alt=""
   src="http://www.googleadservices.com/pagead/conversion/1043170427/?value=0&amp;label=MNPiCLPEnAMQ-
   4i28QM&amp;guid=ON&amp;script=0"/>
   </div>
   </noscript>

   Once you've added the Conversion Tracking code to your site, it can take up to 24 hours before conversions appear in
   your AdWords account.

   Done
```

Figure 12-6. Generate the tracking code

Top Conversions
  Top conversions for the account

Assist Clicks and Impressions
  Shows performance based on how many assisting clicks and impressions there are
  for each keyword, ad group, or campaign

Assisted Conversions
  Shows performance based on how many conversions were assisted by each keyword, ad group, or campaign

First Click Analysis
  Filters conversion reports based on what was first clicked leading to the conversion

---

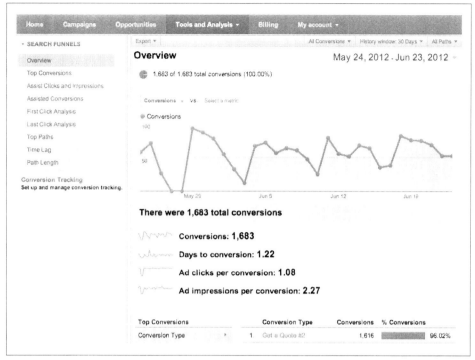

Figure 12-7. Search Funnels reports

Last Click Analysis
Filters conversion reports based on what was last clicked prior to the conversion

Top Paths
Shows the sequence of keywords clicked by customers prior to converting and the frequency with which each path occurred

Time Lag
Shows how long it took customers to convert after first seeing the ad

Path Length
Shows how many ad clicks or impressions it took customers to get to conversion

Google Analytics

This section is a nod to Google Analytics.

Google Analytics is a free, enterprise-class web analytics platform. AdWords users have unlimited usage; non-AdWords users can track up to 5 million pageviews per month.

Google Analytics provides reports on site usage, the content on your website, social media interaction, mobile usage, conversions and—most relevantly—your advertising

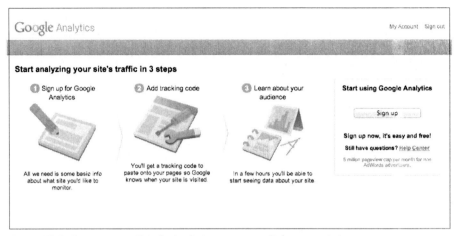

Figure 12-8. Create a new Google Analytics account or link to an existing account

campaigns. Integrated with AdWords, Google Analytics shows post-click data that can help measure the effectiveness of your advertising campaigns. The reports show performance on Search, the Google Display Network, and mobile.

Unlike AdWords reporting, Google Analytics reports on all traffic to your website, from all sources. Use the reports to get a complete picture of how people and finding your site and what they do when they get there. The reports help you find the most profitable sources of traffic, whether that be AdWords, other SEM platforms, email campaigns, and more.

If your digital advertising campaigns span multiple channels, like AdWords, email, social media campaigns, and others, it's helpful to understand how they work together. Multi-Channel Funnels reports show how they work together, allowing you to optimize campaigns across your entire program.

SSo where to begin? Let's cover the basic steps for setting up Google Analytics and connecting it to your AdWords account. After that, explore online resources and Justin Cutroni's Google Analytics (O'Reilly, 2010).

Setting Up Google Analytics

The easiest way to create an Analytics account is to start from the "Tools and Analysis" tab in your AdWords account. Click the link labeled "Google Analytics" to access the setup wizard.

1. If you plan to create a new Google Analytics account, click "Create my free Google Analytics account" and then Continue, shown in Figure 12-8.

2. Next, specify an identifying name for the account, the website's URL, country and time zone. Check the box agreeing to the terms and conditions and click "Create Account" shown in Figure 12-9

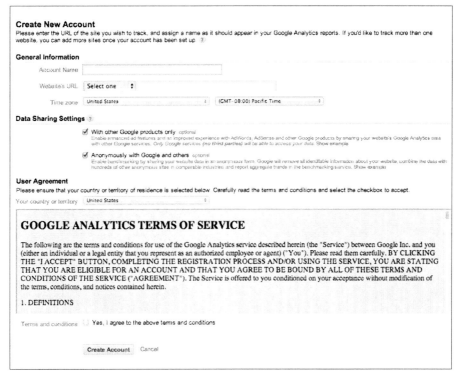

Figure 12-9. Create a new Google Analytics account

3. Now you are in the Admin area for the new account, shown in Figure 12-10. From here you can get the tracking code, give other people access to the reports, set up goals (another way to track conversions), and more.

   There is a section labeled "What are you tracking?" Be sure to check the box labeled "AdWords campaigns" to enable auto-tagging. Auto-tagging automatically appends a tracking ID to AdWords destination URLs. This ID allows Analytics to report details, including the campaign, keyword, and cost for the click.

   Alternatively, you can manually tag Destination URLs with the Google Analytics URL Builder (*http://goo.gl/DejGh*).

   The tracking code is available in this admin area. Be sure to place the code after the close head tag on every page of your website for accurate reporting.

After tagging your pages, you see reports like Figure 12-11 within 24 hours.

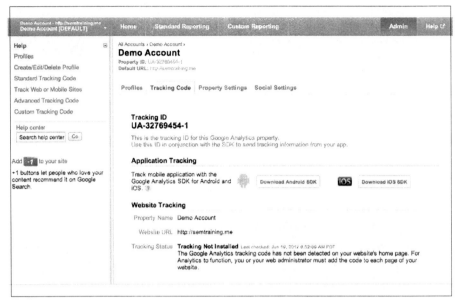

Figure 12-10. Mange your Google Analytics account in the Admin area

 Similar to conversion tracking, Google Analytics can track conversion events, called goals. With Analytics reports, you can see a funnel visualization report, showing how visitors progressed on your site toward a conversion. The funnel is the path you expect visitors to take; tagging these pages shows where visitors abandoned the path.

You can import Google Analytics goals into AdWords via Conversion Tracking.

To learn more about Google Analytics, visit the Help Center at *http://goo.gl/BEPvQ*. This section offers links to many resources, including:

- Help Center
- Google Analytics Blog
- User Forum
- YouTube Channel
- Developer Resources

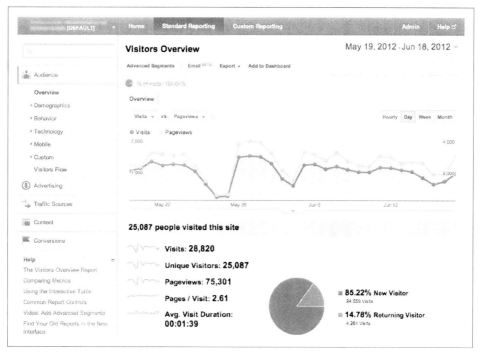

Figure 12-11. A Google Analytics report

CHAPTER 13

Agency Topics

Managing AdWords Accounts for Clients

I meet many small marketing agencies and freelancers interested in adding AdWords account management to their list of services. In many cases, managing a client's pay-per-click campaigns is a natural extension of their existing marketing services.

But how do you get started? There are many ways to manage accounts, from manual edits to sophisticated third-party bid and client management platforms. These decisions will be driven by how many clients you have, the size of their budgets, and your own resources.

If you're not sure where to begin, just begin. This chapter introduces some to-dos, tools, and programs to help you get started.

The My Client Center

The most common new agency mistake is account structure. Here's the scenario. An agency decides to offer AdWords consulting, and creates an AdWords account to manage clients. As new clients sign on, the agency creates a campaign for each new client in the account. This makes it efficient for the agency to manage clients, but it creates huge problems down the line. For example:

- Access and confidentiality: if all clients are associated with the same account, the data cannot be kept confidential. If client A logs in to the account, she can see the campaigns for clients B, C, and D.

- Quality Score: each account accrues a quality score based on the overall performance of the campaigns within. Based on performance disparities between campaigns, clients might benefit and some might be hurt by the performance differences.

- Transfer and history: AdWords accounts cannot be transferred to different accounts. Once the account is created, that primary login cannot be changed. So, if a client decides to take account management in-house or transfer to a different vendor, they cannot take the account with them unless you surrender that login.

You can make a copy of the client's campaign and place it in a different AdWords account using AdWords Editor.

Bottom line: create a separate AdWords account for each client, with a login email address you can transfer if the relationship terminates. I setup a new Gmail address for each new client account, or request a generic login email from the client (i.e., adwords@clientcompany.com). Remember, an email address can be associated with a single AdWords account.

To make management easier, Google offers a tool called the My Client Center (MCC), shown in Figure 13-1. The MCC is a free umbrella account used for managing multiple AdWords accounts, referred to as managed accounts or child accounts. MCC's are used by SEM agencies, bid managers and advertisers with multiple accounts to streamline management.

Using an MCC, you login once and have access to all linked accounts, including other MCCs. Once logged in, you see high-level statistics for all managed accounts. You can access reporting tools to run across accounts and download data. Within the MCC, you can create and link accounts.

Another advantage: if a potential client asks for a review of their AdWords account, I request their 10-digit customer ID. Then, I request access to the account via the MCC. Once a client accepts the invitation, a link to that account appears in the MCC list. I did not have to ask for the account password, and the client has the option to terminate access. In addition, any changes I make are recognizable in the My Change History area, labeled with my MCC name.

The MCC is a requirement for taking advantage of other AdWords features, including the AdWords API and joining the Engage program.

To get started, visit *http://goo.gl/YM6EV* to create a My Client Center account.

Manager Defined Spend

Another nice feature available for MCC holders is the option to use a Manager Defined Spend (MDS).

With MDS, you manage budgets for a group of clients through the MCC. The budgets you choose can be changed via the MCC dashboard. Unlike AdWords, the managed accounts in the group are no longer individually billed; the MCC holder is billed for all in one Manager Order-level monthly invoice.

To set this up, you need to work with an AdWords representative to set up a Manager Defined Order (previously called a "standing order"). Once the MDO is created and processed, MDS is set to go.

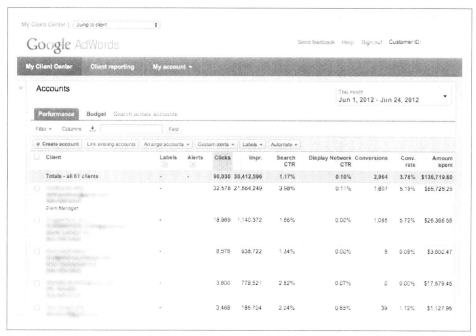

Figure 13-1. The My Client Center streamlines managing multiple accounts

To learn more, visit *http://goo.gl/uYJaZ*.

Third Party Policy

If you offer AdWords consulting services, you are subject to Google's third party policy. The policy specifies a list of rules that agencies and other third parties must follow. There are eight key points to the policy:

1. **You must provide basic reporting**

   Agencies should provide AdWords clients with monthly data on AdWords costs, clicks, and impressions at the account level (at minimum).

2. **You might have to publish a Google Disclosure Notice**

   If 80 percent or more of your clients spend less than $1,000 USD (or local currency equivalent) per month on AdWords, you're required to share a disclosure document. The document must be published on your website in an easily discoverable location. Prior to a onboarding a new client or renewing a contract, agencies are required to inform clients about disclosure.

3. **Do not engage in unclear, deceptive, or harassing sales practices**

   This also includes repeatedly cold calling potential clients, disregarding email opt-opt policies, or excess sales pressure.

4. **Do not misrepresent your relationship to Google**

   Agencies cannot claim to be Google, have special access to Google, ad positions, discounts, or special pricing. Agencies cannot claim to have a special relationship with Google, unless authorized (for example, a Google Certified Partner).

5. **Do not make improper guarantees about Google**

   You have to set accurate expectations for clients. For example you can't sell permanent AdWords positions or claim that you guarantee top placement.

6. **Do not violate Google's branding guidelines**

   Don't mess with Google's trademark. If you are given permission to publish a Google badge, follow the rules.

7. **Do not improperly use AdWords accounts, or AdWords marketing or sales material**

   You can't rebrand Google's sales material as your own, add multiple clients to a single account, sell or trade AdWords coupons, or maliciously delete client accounts.

8. **Don't ever do these**

   No phishing, no pretending to be Google, and the final catch-all: "Other actions that Google deems to be imminently harmful to Google's advertisers or users."

To read the policy in it's entirety, visit *http://goo.gl/rqWEV*.

AdWords Editor

One of the most useful tools for account management is AdWords Editor, shown in Figure 13-2. This standalone application makes it easy to make bulk changes to AdWords accounts, changes that could take hours or weeks in the interface.

To use the Editor, start by downloading it here: www.google.com/adwordseditor (*http://goo.gl/NBTdX*). The Editor is compatible with Macs and PCs. For Windows, it requires 2000/XP/Vista/7. For Macs, it requires OS X(10.4+). You need to install the software on your computer to use it.

So, what are the big advantages of the Editor? First of all, you don't need to be online to use it. Once you have the most recent copy of an AdWords account, you can make changes offline until it is ready to go live. Working this way is much faster than making changes through the interface, and it enables you to complete client work when you're on an airplane, sitting at a ball game, or killing time on the family road trip (yes, I've done that).

Most components of the online interface are available in Editor. You can manage keywords, placements, ads (except video ads), ad groups, ad extensions (sitelinks and location extensions only), and campaigns. Some features, like advanced geotargeting, are best suited for the online interface.

With AdWords Editor, you can copy and paste pieces of accounts within an account, and to other accounts. You can copy anything: keywords, ad groups, campaigns, even entire accounts.

Let's talk about bulk changes. Your client's account might include 200 ads in dozens of ad groups. You learn that the website's domain name is changing, or a published price is changing. This means you might need to edit some or all of your ads. In the online interface, you have to edit ads one by one. With Editor, you can quickly find all ads that need to be changed and run a single search and replace to make the update.

Another perk: unlike the online interface, Editor offers an advanced search feature to identify sections of the account that fit multiple criteria, like text, bids, match type, status and performance statistics.

AdWords Editor provides a handy backup feature for client accounts. If you'd like to store previous versions of client accounts, go to File>Export Backup (AEA) to save a dated copy of the account. The online interface shows changes in the Change History tool, but does not offer a revert option. You can use a saved AEA file in an emergency.

AdWords Editor is also useful for collaboration. If you work with a team, you can leave notes on sections of the account, using the comments feature. When you're ready to share the work, export the account under File>Export changes for sharing (AES) and email the file to collaborators. They can open the AES file in AdWords editor and review all items with comments.

The list of benefits goes on. You can create draft campaigns, and take advantage of tools like "Find duplicate keyword," the "Keyword Grouper" and "Keyword Opportunities."

To access accounts in Editor, you need the AdWords username and password. If you manage client accounts via an MCC, you can use the MCC credentials to login, and all managed accounts will be accessible. You can open multiple MCC accounts, and easily toggle between accounts.

 To learn more about using AdWords Editor, visit the Help Center at *http://goo.gl/pzcNd*.

Google Engage

Once your MCC is set up, it's a great idea to join Google's Engage program. Engage is a free program designed to help small agencies manage AdWords accounts for clients.

Start by applying for membership at *http://goo.gl/MHXjd* (United States and Canada only). You will need to login with your Google account, and fill out an online application with questions about the AdWords accounts you manage (or plan to manage),

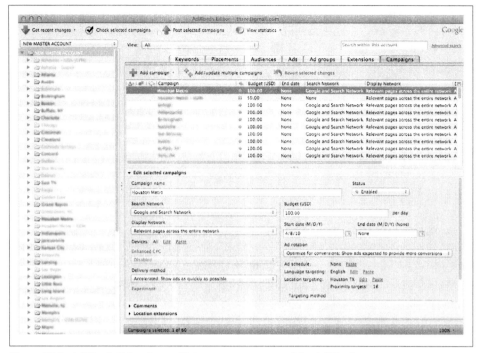

Figure 13-2. AdWords Editor is an efficient management tool for AdWords accounts

your business, and your marketing experience. A Google representative will call in the next few days to go over your application and let you know if you've been accepted into the program.

Once accepted, you have access to the Engage portal. The portal has some nice advantages. You can:

- Request AdWords coupons for onboarding new clients.
- Apply for free Google Certified Partner exam vouchers (up to $200 certification value).
- Access marketing tools like case studies to help pitch clients on your services.
- Register for free training events with Google certified trainers.

Google Certification

Once you've joined Google Engage, the next step is to become a Google Certified Partner. This is one of the best ways to demonstrate proficiency and establish credibility with prospective clients.

There are two levels of certification:

- Google Certified Partners

Figure 13-3. The AdWords Certified Partner badge

- Google Certified Individuals

Becoming a Certified Partner authorizes you to associate a badge (shown in Figure 13-3) with your company in print and online materials. Your company can also opt into Google's Partner Search database: *http://goo.gl/S3ti1*.

To become a Certified Partner, a company must have an MCC in use for at least 90 days. During that 90 day period, the company must manage a minimum of $10,000 USD (spent from accounts in the MCC, starting from the day the AdWords accounts were linked).

At least one person from the company must pass two certification exams. The Google Advertising Fundamentals Exam is required; in addition, she must pass at least one of the following:

- Search Advertising Advanced Exam
- Display Advertising Advanced Exam
- Reporting & Analysis Advanced Exam

To become a Certified Individual, you do not need an MCC or have a minimum spend. You need to pass two of the four exams, and agree to the AdWords Terms and Conditions.

To get started, join the program here: *http://goo.gl/VMxG2*. This area is separate from the MCC and the Engage portal. From here, you can manage your company profile, see your partner status, and access marketing tools.

If you have not taken the qualification exams, your status will be unverified. When you're ready to take the exams (with the free vouchers you requested from the Engage portal), go to the "My Exams" section (under the Individual tab). From here, you get your candidate ID, required for taking the exams. You can also access study materials (*http://goo.gl/Qnazn*), see a history of previously taken tests, or launch the test center, which is administered through the Google Testing Center (*http://goo.gl/zqad1*).

These tests are specific—some colleagues, even experienced marketers, have difficulty passing. If you have not actively managed an AdWords account it's a good idea to do that before taking the exam. If you're a seasoned pro, you may want to review the study materials to familiarize yourself with the most up-to-date information.

Passing scores are as follows:

- Google Advertising Fundamentals Exam: 85 percent
- Search Advertising Advanced Exam: 80 percent
- Reporting and Analysis Exam: 75 percent
- Display Exam: 70 percent

And Finally, Good Luck!

If you made it to the end of this book, it's time to grab a cocktail and relax! I hope this information helps you succeed with AdWords, whether for your own company or for clients.

If you're not reading this book within one week of publication, chances are something changed. To help you keep on top things, here are a few websites with useful information:

- Inside AdWords (*http://goo.gl/50drO*)
- Google Agency Blog (http://goo.gl/unKHy/ (*http://goo.gl/unKHy*))
- Google Official Blog (*http://goo.gl/TZGlx*)
- Google Ad Innovations (*http://goo.gl/jbSK4*)
- Search Engine Watch (*http://goo.gl/z7Fja*)
- SemTraining.me (my blog) (*http://goo.gl/1FIOe*)

Happy advertising! And may the odds be ever in your favor.

Glossary

The following glossary should help you understand the most commonly used terms in AdWords and online marketing. For a complete list, visit the AdWords Glossary at *http://goo.gl/H3Ume*.

Ad Group

An ad group is part of the AdWords account structure. Each ad group defines a set of keywords or placements (or both), the default bid (or individual bids for keywords and placements), and the associated ad creative. Campaigns may include up to 20,000 ad groups. Successful AdWords accounts typically have many ad groups focused on specific themes. The relevancy of the keywords to the ad text in each ad group is an important factor in the AdWords Quality Score calculation.

See also **Campaign**.

Ad Rank

Ad rank represents your "place" in the AdWords auction. The highest-ranking ad wins first place, and therefore the first ad position on the page. The formula for determining Ad Rank is: *Ad Rank = f(Quality Score, Max CPC bid)*.

See also **Maximum Cost-Per-Click (Max CPC), Quality Score**.

AdSense

AdSense allows website publishers to display AdWords ads. AdSense members are part of the Google Display Network. Publishers earn revenue when visitors view or click on the ads. When displaying ads with AdSense for content, publishers receive 68 percent of the amount Google collects from advertisers. When using AdSense for search, publishers receive 51 percent of the amount collected from advertisers. See http://www.google.com/adsense (*http://goo.gl/T3nEV*).

AdWords Application Programming Interface (API)

Allows developers to build applications that interact directly with AdWords. These applications enable efficient management of complex AdWords accounts. The API can automate keyword generation, dynamic ad text and destination URLs, integrate AdWords data with inventory systems, and develop custom tools to manage accounts. The AdWords API SOAP interface is supported by many programming languages, including Java, PHP, Python, .NET, Perl, Ruby, and JavaScript. Visit the API microsite at *http://goo.gl/ebWjC* to learn more.

AdWords Certified Partner

Non-Google employees certified by Google to manage AdWords accounts. To become qualified, partners must demonstrate an indepth understanding of AdWords by passing exams, and manage at least $10,000 USD in advertiser spend through a My Client Center within 90 days. Partner must have at least one individually qualified employee and agree to Google's terms and conditions. Certified partners can be located via Google's Partner Search (*http://goo.gl/pmr7u*). To learn more about the program, visit the Google Certification Program microsite (*http://goo.gl/K5QvI*).

See also **My Client Center (MCC)**.

AdWords

AdWords is the name of Google's advertising platform. There is no such thing as an "AdWord."

AdWords Editor

A free, separate Google application that allows advertisers to manage AdWords accounts offline. It offers significant advantages, including the ability to save backups, collaborate with a group, make bulk edits efficiently, and easily identify duplicate keywords. Download the Editor at Google.com/intl/en/adwordseditor/ (*http://goo.gl/kWBtR*).

Automatic Placements

A placement is a place on the Google Display Network where AdWords ads can appear. A placement is typically a website or a page on a website. Automatic placements are those identified by Google, based on keywords in an ad group. AdWords uses contextual targeting to identify appropriate placements to display ads.

See also **Google Display Network (GDN)**, **Managed Placements**.

Average Cost-Per-Click (Avg. CPC)

The average amount paid each time someone clicks an ad. Average CPC is determined by totaling the cost of all clicks and dividing it by the number of clicks received.

Average Position (Avg. Pos.)

A statistic attributed to each keyword that indicates the average position of an ad on a search result page when triggered by that keyword. Position 1 is the highest position on the first page of search results, relative to other advertisers. There is no bottom position. Keywords with an average position of 1–8 generally display ads on the first page of search results. Keywords with an average position of 9–16 generally display ads on the second page and beyond. An average position of 1.6 means the ad usually appears in position 1 or 2. Average positions are not fixed; they vary depending on various performance factors, including the keyword that triggers the ad.

Bid Simulator

An AdWords feature that recalculates auctions from the last seven days to show how a keyword might have performed with different Max CPC bids. Bid Simulator uses internal auction data, including Quality Score, to estimate where ads would have appeared and how frequently they would have been clicked with different bids. The simulator estimates click, cost, and impression data for Google Search and the Search Partners, not the Google Display Network.

See also **Maximum Cost-Per-Click (Max CPC)**.

Bounce Rate

Bounce rate is the percentage of single-page visits to a website.

Broad Match Keyword

Describes the default AdWords keyword match type. A broad match keyword can trigger ads when a searcher's query matches the keyword, includes the keyword, or is a variation of it. Keyword variations include synonyms, singulars and plurals, and variants.

Campaign

A campaign is part of the AdWords account structure. Each account can contain up to 10,000 campaigns (including enabled and paused campaigns). Campaigns control administrative settings, including the geographic areas where ads can display, the default language, ad distribution preferences and devices, and the daily budget.

See also **Ad Group**.

Click

A click is counted when someone clicks on an AdWords ad after a search or when coming across an ad on a website in the Google

Display Network. A phone call initiated from an ad on a mobile device also counts as an AdWords click. With the pay-per-click model, advertisers pay when people click on their ads.

Clickthrough Rate (CTR)

Clickthrough rate is the number of clicks an ad receives divided by the number of times it is displayed (impressions). CTR is the most important factor in the AdWords Quality Score calculation.

See also Quality Score.

Conversion

When a click on an ad results in a desirable behavior by the visitor. Conversions are the true measure of success for advertisers. Example conversions include an online sale, a signup, a form submission, or a download. Advertisers can track conversions using Conversion Tracking, found in the "Tools and Analysis" tab, or by setting up goals in Google Analytics.

See also Google Analytics (GA).

Conversion Optimizer

An AdWords bidding option that uses conversion tracking data to dynamically manage bids toward a CPA goal. Advertisers still pay for clicks, but do not adjust bids manually; Conversion Optimizer automatically finds the optimal equivalent cost-per-click bid by calculating a predicted conversion rate for each auction.

See also CPA Bidding.

Conversion Rate

Conversions divided by total clicks. If conversion tracking is set up, AdWords shows one-per-click and many-per-click conversion rates. Many-per-click can credit a keyword with more than one conversion per click, resulting in a conversion rate that exceeds 100 percent.

Cost-Per-Click (CPC)

A pricing model where advertisers pay for clicks on ads, usually at a price they specify. CPC is also called pay-per-click (PPC).

See also Pay-Per-Click (PPC).

Cost-Per-Conversion

The total cost divided by conversions. This metric can report costs for 1-per-click and many-per-click conversions.

CPA Bidding

Stands for cost-per-acquisition (CPA). This bidding model is available for advertisers using Conversion Optimizer, which allows maximum or target CPA bids for each ad group. A maximum CPA bid specifies the upper limit advertisers are willing to pay for conversions. Target CPA specifies the average amount advertisers are willing to pay for conversions.

See also Conversion Optimizer.

CPM Bidding

Stands for cost-per-thousand impressions. This pricing model is available for placement-targeted campaigns on the Google Display Network only. Advertisers specify the maximum amount they're willing to pay for every 1,000 ad impressions.

See also Placement Targeted Campaign.

Customer ID (CID)

A 10-digit number used to identify each AdWords account. The CID is found at the top right corner of an AdWords account, formatted like this: xxx-xxx-xxxx. When viewing an account via a My Client Center account (MCC), the CID (labeled Client ID) appears in the left corner, and the MCC's Manager ID is listed in the right corner.

See also My Client Center (MCC).

Delivery Method

A campaign setting that determines how quickly ads are shown each day. The default, standard delivery, distributes ads as evenly as possible within the budget, over a 24-hour period. Accelerated delivery displays ads as quickly as possible until the daily budget is spent. With accelerated delivery, ads stop serving until the next day.

Destination URL

The web page that people actually end up on after clicking on an ad.

Dimension

In AdWords, a way to look at data beyond total numbers in a single campaign or ad group. A dimension provides insight into what happens across the entire account on particular days of the week, times of the day, parts of the world, etc. These reports are accessible from the Dimensions roll-up tab.

Display Ad Builder

A tool in an AdWords account that provides templates for creating image and video ads. Advertisers select templates and customize the content with text, images, and links.

Display URL

The website address that's displayed with an ad.

Distribution Preference

A campaign setting that determines which AdWords networks can display ads. The networks include Google Search, the Search Partners, and the Google Display Network.

See also Search Network or Search Partners, Google Display Network (GDN).

Double-Serving

Describes displaying more than one ad for the same company on a single search results page. Google does not permit advertisers and affiliates to double-serve ads across multiple accounts for the same or similar businesses or the same or similar keywords.

Exact Match Keyword

A match type that restricts the delivery of an ad to a search query that matches a keyword exactly, character-for-character (now expanded to singulars, plurals, misspellings, and stemmings, but no additional words). To specify exact match, surround the keyword with square brackets, as in [example exact match keyword]. In this case, only a search for example exact match keyword is eligible to trigger an ad.

First Page Bid Estimate

An estimate intended to show advertisers what bid is required to display an ad on the first page of Google's search results. The estimate is based on a search query that matches the keyword exactly. It considers the keyword's Quality Score and advertiser competition.

Frequency Capping

A campaign setting applicable to the Google Display Network only. Frequency capping limits the number of times ads can be shown to a unique person in a specified period of time. Use frequency capping to limit the number of impressions allowed per day, per week, or per month. The cap can apply to ads, ad groups, or campaigns.

Google Account

A single email and password used to access multiple Google services, including AdWords, Gmail, Google Groups, Google Alerts, Google Product Search, and Google Apps. A Gmail account is already a Google account; any email address can be used to create a free Google account. If you are not sure if an email address is already a Google account, use the password recovery feature (*http://goo.gl/009N*) to see if Google recognizes the email address. To create a Google account, visit *http://goo.gl/dl0NF*.

Google Analytics (GA)

A free analytics program that shows how people found a website and what they did there. Google Analytics (GA) integrates with AdWords, showing activity on the site derived from specific campaigns, ad groups, and keywords.

Google Display Network (GDN)

An advertising network that allows AdWords advertisers to show ads on websites, called placements. The GDN accepts text, image, video, and rich media ad formats. Advertisers can target ads based on keyword themes, topics, and specific web pages.

See also Automatic Placements, Managed Placements.

Impression

The number of times an ad is displayed, whether it is clicked or not.

Impression Share

A metric that represents the percentage of times ads were shown out of the total available impressions for which ads were eligible to appear. Eligibility is based on the ads' targeting settings, approval statuses, and bids.

Keyword

A keyword is a word or phrase that can trigger an ad. Keywords are limited to 10 words and 80 characters, including spaces. Each ad group can contain 5,000 keywords, including negative keywords.

Keyword Insertion

A technique used to dynamically update ad text with keywords from an ad group. The technique is also called Dynamic Keyword Insertion (DKI) and wildcard. To use DKI, place a tag in the ad text where the keyword should appear when it triggers an ad. Ads are still subject to AdWords advertising policies.

Landing Page

The web page searchers see after clicking an AdWords ad. The landing page is specified in the Destination URL field when writing an ad.

Managed Placements

Specific sites or pages in the Google Display Network where ads can appear. A campaign can include both automatic and managed placements or be restricted to managed placements only. This campaign setting is specified in the Networks section of the campaign settings. Placements can be found via the Placement Tool in the "Tools and Analysis" tab.

Many-Per-Click Conversions

A metric that records a conversion for every ad click resulting in a conversion within 30 days. It can count multiple conversions per click.

See also One-Per-Click Conversions.

Match Type

Determines how closely the search query must match the keyword to be eligible to trigger an ad.

See also Broad Match Keyword, Phrase Match Keyword, Exact Match Keyword, Negative Keyword.

Maximum Cost-Per-Click (Max CPC)

A bid in the AdWords auction, specifying the highest amount an advertiser is willing to pay for a click on an ad.

Maximum Cost-Per-Phone Call (Max CPP)

Available for advertisers using Call Metrics, Max CPP specifies the bid, the highest price an advertiser is willing to pay each time a visitor manually dials the Google forwarding number shown with ads on desktop and tablet devices.

Metric

As applied to an AdWords account, any measurement used to gauge performance, such as impressions, clickthrough rate, cost-per-conversion, etc.

My Change History

A feature that shows changes made to an AdWords account, back to January 1, 2006. View changes by time or types of changes. If multiple users with separate logins have access to the account, the feature shows who made the changes.

My Client Center (MCC)

A free umbrella account used to manage multiple AdWords accounts. An MCC allows a single login to access all managed accounts, view selected statistics across accounts, and run reports across multiple managed accounts. MCC owners can create new accounts and link existing AdWords accounts. MCC accounts can link to five additional MCCs. An MCC is a requirement for becoming an AdWords Certified Partner. Sign up at *http://goo.gl/CzHr7*.

Negative Keyword

A word or phrase that prevents ads from appearing when included in the searcher's query. Negative keywords applied at the ad group level count toward the 5,000 keyword limit. Advertisers can apply up to 10,000 negative keywords at the campaign level, per campaign.

One-Per-Click Conversions

An account metric that records a conversion for every ad click resulting in a conversion within 30 days. It counts one conversion per unique user, per ad click. If the same user completes more than one conversion after the single ad click, conversions after the first will not count.

See also Many-Per-Click Conversions.

Pay-Per-Click (PPC)

A pricing model where advertisers pay for clicks on ads, usually at a price they specify. PPC is also called cost-per-click (CPC).

See also Cost-Per-Click (CPC).

Phrase Match Keyword

A match type that restricts the delivery of an ad to a search query that matches a keyword exactly, character-for-character, but allows additional words before and after the keyword. To specify phrase match, surround the keyword with quotes, as in "`example phrase match keyword.`" In this scenario, a search for `example phrase match keyword` is eligible to trigger an ad. A search for `another example phrase match keyword here` could also trigger an ad, because the keyword phrase is intact. A search for `phrase match keyword example` cannot trigger an ad.

Placements

Locations on the Google Display Network where ads can appear. Placements include websites, subsets of websites (such as a selection of pages from that site), or individual ad units.

See also Automatic Placements, Managed Placements.

Placement Targeted Campaign

A campaign that displays ads on the Google Display Network, using managed placements only. This setting is selected from the Networks section in the campaign settings.

Placement targeted campaigns have the option to use CPM bidding.

See also CPM Bidding, Automatic Placements, Managed Placements.

Quality Score

There are several Quality Scores associated with an AdWords account. The score that matters most in the AdWords auction is at the keyword level. Every keyword in an AdWords account has a separate Quality Score. It's a dynamic variable calculated every time a search query matches the keyword. In an account, it's represented as a number between 1 and 10. The higher the Quality Score, the better. Scores from 7 to 10 are great; 5 to 6 are OK; and 1 to 4 mean the keyword may have trouble winning the ad auction. Quality Score is an important component of the auction, used to determine ad rank and actual cost per click.

See also Ad Rank, Clickthrough Rate (CTR).

Return on Investment (ROI)

The ratio of the cost of advertising to the profit generated from conversions. ROI indicates the value to your business gained in comparison to the advertising costs. To calculate ROI, take revenue from sales, subtract advertising costs, then divide by total advertising costs: (Revenue − Cost) ÷ Cost. To get the best results from AdWords, it's important to determine the ROI per keyword via conversion tracking, Google Analytics, or both. Once you know the value of each keyword, bid strategically, focusing on your best performers and cutting back on poor performers. These adjustments improve your return on investment.

Search Network or Search Partners

An advertising network available to AdWords advertisers made up of a group of websites that use Google's search technology. The Search Partners are subject to change; as of this writing, partners include AOL.com and Google properties like Google Maps, Google Groups, Google Images, Google News, and others. Ads are keyword targeted and limited to text. The one exception is Google Images; the text ad is accompanied by a 160 × 160 pixel image. To display ads on the Search Network, the campaign must also be opted into Google Search.

Text Ad

The primary type of AdWords ad, text ads show on Google search, the Search Partners, and the Google Display Network. Ads include 25 characters for the headline, two 35-character description lines, and 35 characters for a Display URL. Each ad includes a destination URL with a 1,024 character limit.

Top-Ranked Ad

Ads that appear above Google's organic search results, in the center well of the search results page. To qualify, ads must exceed a Quality Score and bid threshold determined by the AdWords algorithm (but not published).

View-Through Conversion

View-through conversions show the number of online conversions that happened within 30 days after a person saw, but *did not click*, a display ad on the Google Display Network. If a click on a GDN display ad precedes the conversion, the conversion is treated as a click-conversion. View-through conversions are not reported for text ads on the GDN or search campaigns. The account must have conversion tracking enabled, and Google Analytics goals are not compatible.

AdWords counts all conversions *not associated* with a click and attributes them back to the last impression in the last 30 days. Consequently, a single impression can be associated with multiple view-through conversions. In cases where a conversion follows both a search click and a display impression, both a clickthrough conversion and a view-through conversion are counted. View-through reporting uses last click, last impression attribution. So, conversions are credited to the last click on an ad. If there are no clicks in the last 30 days, conversions are credited to the last impression preceding the conversion.

About the Author

Anastasia Holdren is president of SEM Training, providing training and consulting for Google AdWords advertisers. Stasia is one of two Authorized AdWords Seminar Leaders. Working with Google, she piloted the Seminars for Success program in 2006. Since then, she has trained thousands of advertisers around the world.

Stasia has fifteen years of experience managing web technology projects and online marketing programs. Prior to leading the seminars, she was senior vice president for Sitening, the creators of Raven Internet Marketing Tools (*http://goo.gl/R5Jt6*).

Stasia's career began in the Boston area. Before moving to Nashville, she worked for the Boston Globe's website, Boston.com, and a Boston-area web consulting agency.

Stasia has worked for a wide range of clients, including Osram Sylvania, Harvard Business School Executive Education, eMarketer.com, NashvillePost.com, Cannondale, Air Jamaica, the National Federation of Independent Business, Psychiatric Services, and TravelCenters of America.

Stasia earned degrees in English literature and journalism from the University of Massachusetts, Amherst. She lives in Nashville, Tennessee, with her family. When she is not online, she finds balance offline practicing yoga, gardening, and training her dogs.

Get even more for your money.

Join the O'Reilly Community, and register the O'Reilly books you own. It's free, and you'll get:

- $4.99 ebook upgrade offer
- 40% upgrade offer on O'Reilly print books
- Membership discounts on books and events
- Free lifetime updates to ebooks and videos
- Multiple ebook formats, DRM FREE
- Participation in the O'Reilly community
- Newsletters
- Account management
- 100% Satisfaction Guarantee

Signing up is easy:

1. **Go to: oreilly.com/go/register**
2. **Create an O'Reilly login.**
3. **Provide your address.**
4. **Register your books.**

Note: English-language books only

To order books online:
oreilly.com/store

For questions about products or an order:
orders@oreilly.com

To sign up to get topic-specific email announcements and/or news about upcoming books, conferences, special offers, and new technologies:
elists@oreilly.com

For technical questions about book content:
booktech@oreilly.com

To submit new book proposals to our editors:
proposals@oreilly.com

O'Reilly books are available in multiple DRM-free ebook formats. For more information:
oreilly.com/ebooks

O'REILLY®

Spreading the knowledge of innovators   oreilly.com

©2010 O'Reilly Media, Inc. O'Reilly logo is a registered trademark of O'Reilly Media, Inc. 00000

Have it your way.

O'Reilly eBooks

- Lifetime access to the book when you buy through oreilly.com
- Provided in up to four DRM-free file formats, for use on the devices of your choice: PDF, .epub, Kindle-compatible .mobi, and Android .apk
- Fully searchable, with copy-and-paste and print functionality
- Alerts when files are updated with corrections and additions

oreilly.com/ebooks/

Safari Books Online

- Access the contents and quickly search over 7000 books on technology, business, and certification guides
- Learn from expert video tutorials, and explore thousands of hours of video on technology and design topics
- Download whole books or chapters in PDF format, at no extra cost, to print or read on the go
- Get early access to books as they're being written
- Interact directly with authors of upcoming books
- Save up to 35% on O'Reilly print books

See the complete Safari Library at safari.oreilly.com

O'REILLY®

Spreading the knowledge of innovators.

oreilly.com

©2011 O'Reilly Media, Inc. O'Reilly logo is a registered trademark of O'Reilly Media, Inc. 00000

0 1341 1488881 8

DATE DUE	RETURNED
Oct. 26/13	DEC 1 2 2013
APR 2 5 2014	APR 1 7 2014

CPSIA information can be obtained at www.ICGtesting.com
Printed in the USA
LVOW111704270912

300609LV00006B/34/P

9 781449 308384